GREATways to Teach and Learn™

Connect with Reading
Grade 1

Written by

Patricia Pedigo and Roger DeSanti

Edited and produced by
Patricia Pedigo

©2008 Plutarch Publications, Inc. PPI -1001

ISBN 978-1-934990-02-5

GREATways to Teach and Learn: Connect with Reading Grade 1
Published by
Plutarch Publications, Inc.
U.S.A.
Email (for customer service enquires): plutarch_inc@yahoo.com
Copyright© 2008 Plutarch Publications, Inc.

Copyright © 2008, Plutarch Publications, Inc., Mandeville, Louisiana. All rights reserved. The purchase of this material entitles the buyer to reproduce worksheets and activities for classroom use only—not for commercial resale. Reproduction of these materials for an entire school or district is prohibited. No part of this book may be reproduced (except as noted above), stored in a retrieval system, or transmitted in any form or by any means (mechanically, electronically, recording, etc.) without the prior written consent of Plutarch Publications, Inc.

ISBN-13: 978-1-934990-02-5
ISBN-10: 1-934990-02-7

About the series ...

The GREATways to Teach and Learn™ series are books intended to supplement curriculum and textbooks. Over sixty pages of activities presented in each GREATways to Teach and Learn™ book engage the learner in active practice of basic skills required at the appropriate grade level. Activities are designed with various learning styles in mind to include every child in the learning process.

Each book contains two pages of *Quick Cues,* a handy list of important vocabulary, rules, or examples of standards covered in that GREATways to Teach and Learn™ book. The page "How to Use This Book" provides suggestions and ideas for using *Quick Cues* for additional instruction or practice.

GREATways to Teach and Learn™ books are designed to comply with State Curriculum Standards. Although the level at which specific topics are mandated may vary from State to State, many State Curriculum Standards agree on the grade level at which most skills are introduced. The GREATways to Teach and Learn™ series focuses on those standards that are commonly introduced at each grade level. The Score Computation Chart (page 4) and the Standards Competency Chart (page 5) provide a viable means to assess the level at which a child is able to complete each standard presented.

The goal of this series is to provide grade appropriate standards, practice, and application in a straight-forward, easy to understand manner. Appropriate materials and presentation produce comprehension. Practice produces proficiency. Application produces students able to interact with the real world.

About the authors and editor .....

Patricia Pedigo, M.Ed. in elementary education, also earned the Reading Specialist endorsement. She has more than 20 years experience in elementary and junior high classrooms and a passion for working with "learning different" children. Patricia has authored and/or edited 50 instructional books that are used in classrooms across North America.

Roger DeSanti Sr., Ed.D. in Reading and Special Education, is a Professor of Education whose area of expertise is literacy and the learning process. He has over 30 years of classroom experience working with and educating children and their teachers. Roger has over 100 publications, including instructional books that are used in classrooms across North America.

Connect With Reading Grade 1

How to Use This Book 1	**Words in Sentences**
Quick Cues Vocabulary 2	Riddles 41
Quick Cues Vocabulary 3	Riddles 42
Score Computation Chart 4	Riddles 43
Standards Competency Chart 5	Following Directions 44
Concept Building	Following Directions 45
Categorizing 6	Following Directions 46
Categorizing 7	Synonyms in Context 47
Categorizing 8	Synonyms in Context 48
Categorizing 9	Words in Context 49
Categorizing 10	Words in Context 50
Categorizing 11	Words in Context 51
Letter Sound Recognition	Answering Questions 52
Initial Consonant 12	Answering Questions 53
Initial Consonant 13	**Comprehension** *Narrative Stories*
Final Consonant 14	My Pet 54
Final Consonant 15	Playing Together 55
Initial Consonant 16	At the Zoo 56
Initial Consonant 17	My Birthday 57
Initial Consonant 18	Baby Sister 58
Final Consonant 19	Wake Up!.. 59
Final Consonant 20	A Bus Ride 60
Final Consonant 21	**Comprehension** *Expository Stories*
Word Recognition	Plants 61
Word to Picture 22	Matter 62
Word to Picture 23	Senses 63
Word to Picture 24	The Night Sky 64
Picture to Word 25	Weather 65
Picture to Word 26	Friends 66
Word in Context 27	Helping the Family 67
Word in Context 28	A Map of My Bedroom 68
Word in Context 29	A Map of the Park 69
Singular/Plural 30	
Sentence to Picture 31	**Answer Keys**
Sentence to Picture 32	Pages 6 - 9 .... 70 Pages 38 - 41 ... 78
Rhyming 33	Pages 10 - 13... 71 Pages 42 - 45 ... 79
Rhyming 34	Pages 14 - 17 .. 72 Pages 46 - 49 ... 80
Synonyms 35	Pages 18 - 21 .. 73 Pages 50 - 53 ... 81
Synonyms 36	Pages 22 - 25 .. 74 Pages 54 - 57 ... 82
Synonyms 37	Pages 26 - 29... 75 Pages 58 - 61 ... 83
Antonyms 38	Pages 30 - 33 .. 76 Pages 62 - 65 ... 84
Antonyms 39	Pages 34 - 37 .. 77 Pages 66 - 69 ... 85
Antonyms 40	

©2008 Plutarch Publications, Inc. PPI -1001

How to use this book ...

GREATways: Instruction books offer several features designed to enhance the learning process and assist the teacher in assessing the learner's progress. On the next few pages you will find Quick Cues, a Score Computation Chart, a Standards Competency Chart, and recommendations based on the competency level of the learner.

QUICK CUES: This book includes two pages of *Quick Cues* which are important facts at your fingertips. The Quick Cues found on pages two and three of this book lists 160 words that should be part of the basic reading vocabulary of first grade learners. Ways to use these pages are as varied as the number of readers, but here are a few suggestions to get started:
- Have the learner scan a newspaper or magazine and try to find words from the *Quick Cues* list.
- Create a "Book of Words" where the learner places a word from the list on each page and adds an illustration
- Ask the learner to select ten of the words and use them in a story
- List each word on an index card and use them as flashcards. The learner can keep the words that are correctly identified.
- Create a "Word Bank" box where the flashcards can be kept. Have the learner use these words to create sentences or short stories.

SCORE COMPUTATION CHART: This assessment tool can be found on page four of this book. After the learner completes an activity in this book, record the number of correct items on the score computation chart. When all pages for a listed standard have been completed, tally the number of correct answers and record it in the column on the far right (under the total of correct answers possible). Transfer the learner's totals to the chart on page five to find the level of competency.

STANDARDS COMPETENCY CHART: Use the total number correct scores from page four to identify the level at which the learner comprehends/applies the standard. The range of scores within each level (Mastery, Instructional, Basic, and Limited) are approximate indicators of how well the learner understands and can apply each standard. The degree of competency at that level will vary with the score. For example, a score of 41 in Categorizing indicates Mastery, but is close to Instructional and the learner could benefit from more practice with that standard. Recommendations based on the competency level are offered at the bottom of the page.

Quick Cues

First Grade Word List

add	bike	dance	flap
again	bit	dinner	floor
age	bite	dirt	follow
ago	bloom	doctor	full
angry	boat	doll	gate
ant	bone	done	give
around	bow	draw	glass
asleep	bowl	drink	gold
ate	bright	drove	grass
baby	castle	egg	guess
bake	cattle	ever	hand
balloon	cave	eye	head
band	child	face	hear
bark	circle	family	hold
barn	class	farm	hole
been	cloud	fed	hop
below	cold	fell	horse
bench	color	fill	jar
best	cool	final	keep
better	corner	finish	kick

Quick Cues
First Grade Word List

kind	never	right	tiger
king	nice	room	town
kite	nose	rope	toy
kitten	note	sandwich	train
knee	our	secret	try
large	oven	seen	tub
leave	paint	sheep	twig
long	pan	sign	umbrella
loud	part	sister	until
love	party	six	watch
low	paste	snow	wet
luck	picture	song	white
lunch	plan	soon	wind
mail	pot	sound	wise
mail	puppy	soup	wish
mask	push	squirrel	wood
mean	apple	star	yell
might	quack	step	yellow
miss	quiet	tag	zoo
move	ready	teacher	zoom

Score Computation Chart

Connect with Reading

Grade 1

Categorizing											Score
Page number	6	7	8	9	10	11					
# possible	6	6	10	8	8	8					46
# correct											
Initial Consonant											
Page number	12	13	16	17	18						
# possible	16	16	30	30	30						122
# correct											
Final Consonant											
Page number	14	15	19	20	21						
# possible	16	16	30	30	30						122
# correct											
Word Recognition											
Page number	22	23	24	25	26	33	34				
# possible	8	8	8	8	8	40	40				120
# correct											
Words in Context											
Page number	27	28	29	30	31	32	49	50	51		
# possible	6	6	6	6	5	5	15	15	16		79
# correct											
Synonyms											
Page number	35	36	37	47	48						
# possible	10	10	10	15	15						60
# correct											
Antonyms											
Page number	38	39	40								
# possible	10	10	10								30
# correct											
Directions											
Page number	44	45	46								
# possible	15	15	19								49
# correct											
Riddles/Questions											
Page number	41	42	43	52	53						
# possible	5	5	5	7	7						29
# correct											
Narrative Story											
Page number	54	55	56	57	58	59	60	61	62		
# possible	7	7	7	7	7	7	7	7	7		63
# correct											
Expository Story											
Page number	63	64	65	66	67	68	69				
# possible	7	7	7	7	7	7	7				49
# correct											

©2008 Plutarch Publications, Inc. PPI -1001

Standards Competency Chart

Step 1: After the learner completes each page, record the number correct on the Score Computation Chart (page 4). Calculate the total number correct for each standard.

Step 2: Find the learner's score for each standard in the boxes of that row. Mark the box with an X (or the learner's score) to identify the level of competency for that standard. For example, a score of 40 for the standard of Following Directions places the child on the "Instructional" level and a score of 46 would indicate the "Mastery" level.

Step 3: Follow the recommendation guidelines at the bottom of this page.

Standard	Mastery	Instructional	Basic	Limited
Categorizing	46 - 41	40 - 35	34 - 28	27 or below
Initial Consonant	122 - 110	109 - 91	90 - 73	72 or below
Final Consonant	122 - 110	109 - 91	90 - 73	72 or below
Word Recognition	120 - 108	107 - 90	89 - 72	71 or below
Words in Context	79 - 71	70 - 59	58 - 47	46 or below
Synonyms	60 - 54	53 - 45	44 - 36	35 or below
Antonyms	30 - 27	26 - 23	22 - 18	17 or below
Following Directions	49 - 44	43 - 37	36 - 30	29 or below
Riddle/Questions	29 - 26	25 - 22	21 - 17	16 or below
Narrative Passage	63 - 57	56 - 48	47 - 38	37 or below
Expository Passage	49 - 44	43 - 37	36 - 29	28 or below

Recommendation Guidelines

Mastery: The learner is capable of using this standard independently. Move on to the next higher grade level.

Instructional: The learner has a working understanding of the standard, but needs some guided practice on this grade level.

Basic: The learner has minimal grasp of the standard and needs direct instruction and guided practice to apply the concept fully. The learner could benefit from moving one grade level lower for review and extra practice before approaching the standard at this level once again.

Limited: The learner has a limited understanding of the standard and should be moved to the next lower grade level for instruction and practice.

©2008 Plutarch Publications, Inc. PPI -1001

Name _____ Standard: Categorizing

DIRECTIONS:
Look at the pictures in each row. Three of the items belong together. Circle the one that does not belong. Example:

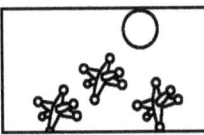 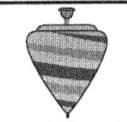  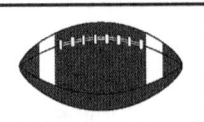

The jacks, top, and ball are all toys. The turtle is not a toy so it doesn't belong in the group.

1.

2.

3.

4.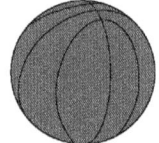

5.

6.

©2008 Plutarch Publications, Inc. PPI-1001

Name _____ Standard: Categorizing

DIRECTIONS:
Look at the pictures in each row. Three of the items belong together. Circle the one that does not belong. Example:

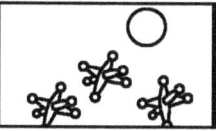   

The jacks, top, and ball are all toys. The turtle is not a toy so it doesn't belong in the group.

1.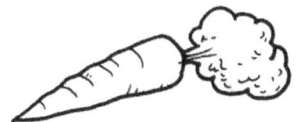

2.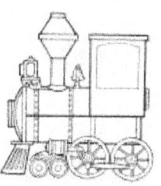

3.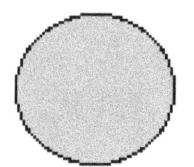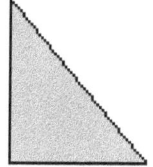

4.

5.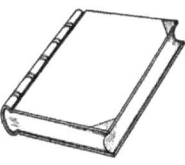

6. a   f   z   2

©2008 Plutarch Publications, Inc. PPI -1001

Name _____   Standard: Categorizing

DIRECTIONS:
Look at the words in each row. Three of the items belong together. Circle the one that does not belong. Example:

hop	jump	(pan)	run
1. white	car	yellow	red
2. one	six	two	been
3. eye	wet	face	nose
4. lost	bike	kite	ball
5. horse	bone	cat	turtle
6. put	park	school	home
7. teacher	mother	sister	rabbit
8. train	very	bus	car
9. many	some	all	leave
10. window	work	door	floor

©2008 Plutarch Publications, Inc. PPI-1001

Name _____   Standard: Categorizing

DIRECTIONS:
Look at the pictures below. Each item on the left goes with one item on the right. Draw lines to match the pictures that belong together.

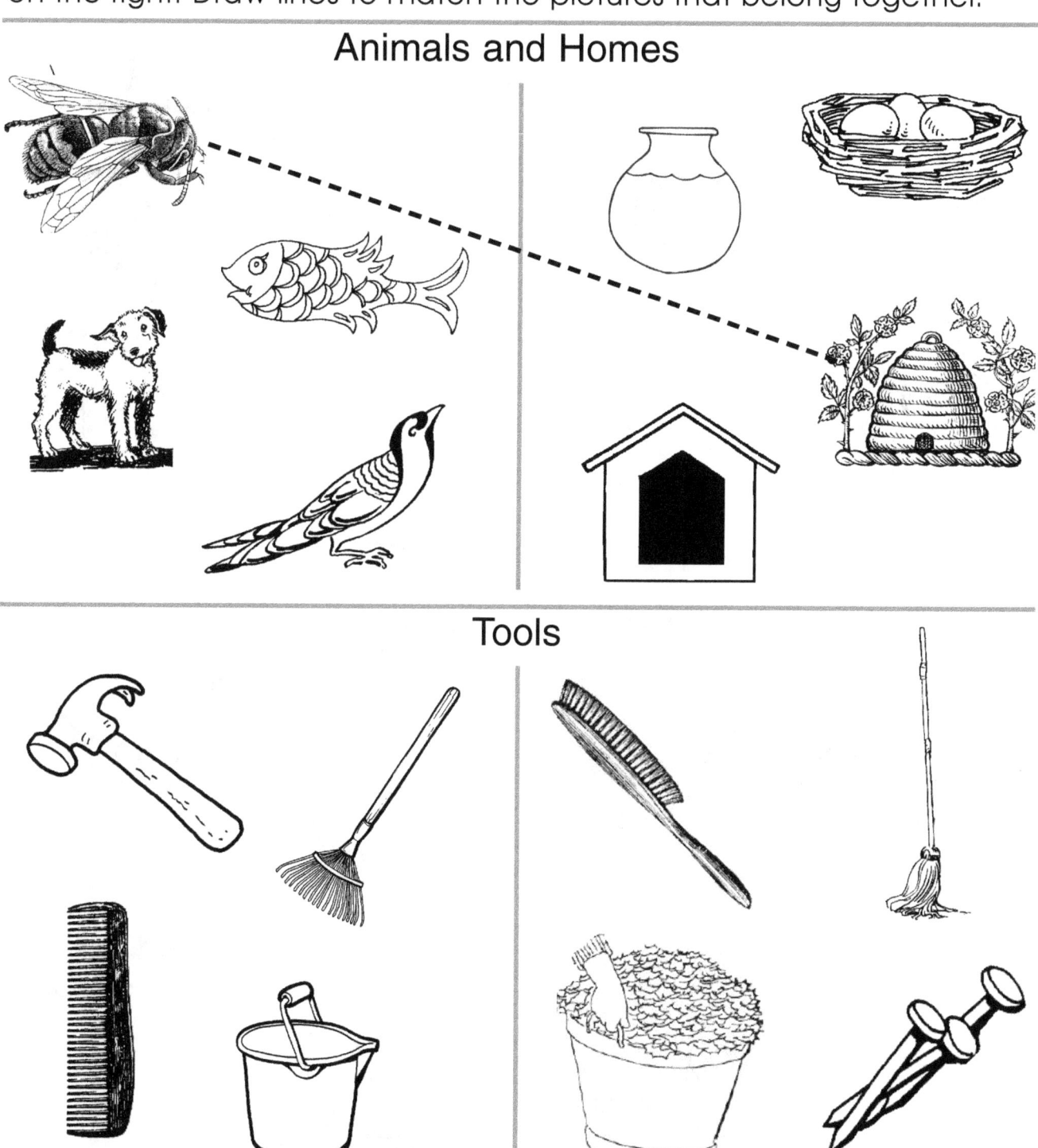

©2008 Plutarch Publications, Inc. PPI-1001

Name _____   Standard: Categorizing

DIRECTIONS:
Look at the pictures below. Each item on the left goes with one item on the right. Match the pictures that belong together. Color the pictures.

Toys

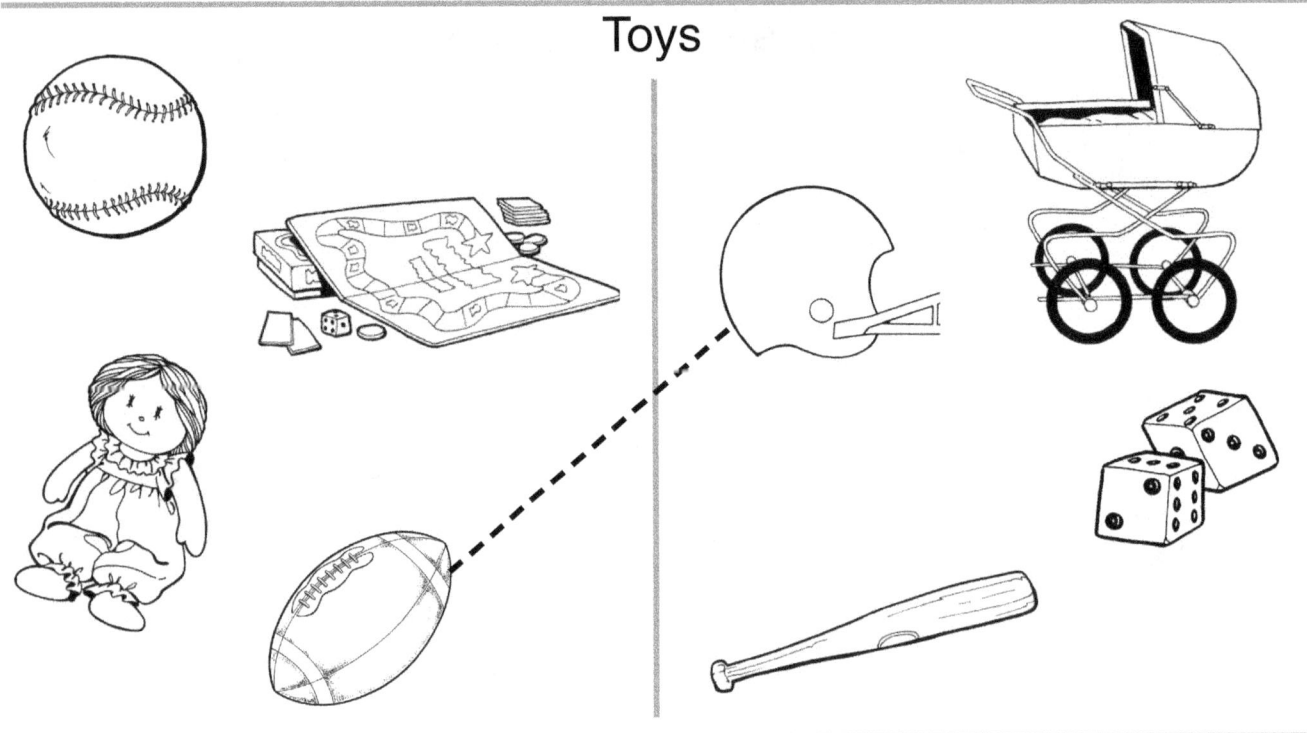

Animals and Babys

©2008 Plutarch Publications, Inc. PPI -1001

Name _____   Standard: Categorizing

DIRECTIONS:
Look at the picture on the left. Circle the pictures of things on the right that belong with the picture on the left. Color the pictures.

barn

doll house

©2008 Plutarch Publications, Inc. PPI-1001

Name _____ Standard: Initial Consonant Recognition

DIRECTIONS: Underline the picture in each box that begins with the letter at the top of that box. Example:

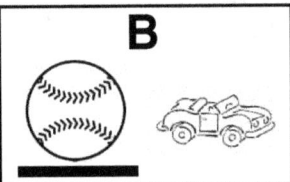

The first one is underlined
Ball begins with **B**
Car begins with **C**

F	N	R	J
C	S	W	M
G	P	T	V
L	K	D	H

©2008 Plutarch Publications, Inc. PPI-1001

Name _____   Standard: Initial Consonant Recognition

DIRECTIONS: Underline the picture in each box that begins with the letter at the top of that box. Example:

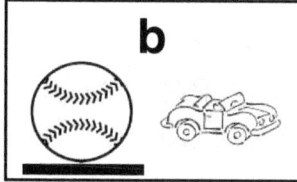

The first one is underlined
  <u>b</u>all begins with **b**
  <u>c</u>ar begins with **c**

m	n	p	r
w	j	b	l
d	g	k	v
h	f	t	s

©2008 Plutarch Publications, Inc. PPI -1001

Name _____ Standard: Final Consonant Recognition

DIRECTIONS: Underline the picture in each box that ends with the letter at the top of that box. Example:

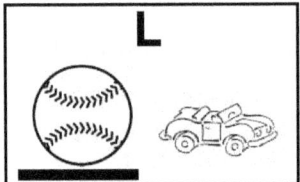

The first one is underlined
BAL<u>L</u> ends with **L**
CA<u>R</u> ends with **R**

| F | N | R | T |
| D | L | S | K |

(Pictures by row:)

Row 1 — **F**: flute, leaf | **N**: clown, mouse | **R**: chair, purse | **T**: bear, ant

Row 2 — **P**: top, sled | **S**: bus, nest | **B**: bat, crib | **M**: match, worm

Row 3 — **G**: log, duck | **D**: hand, pumpkin | **L**: bell, ring | **R**: box, tiger

Row 4 — **B**: balloon, web | **R**: rake, door | **S**: shirt, dress | **K**: book, cup

©2008 Plutarch Publications, Inc. PPI-1001

Name _____   Standard: Final Consonant Recognition

DIRECTIONS: Underline the picture in each box that ends with the letter at the top of that box. Example:

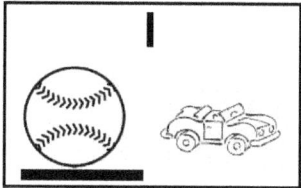

The first one is underlined
ba<u>ll</u> ends with **l**
ca<u>r</u> ends with **r**

f	n	r	p
k	s	d	m
g	b	t	n
l	r	n	g

©2008 Plutarch Publications, Inc. PPI -1001   15

Name _____   Standard: Initial Consonant Recognition

DIRECTIONS: Circle the words in each row that begin with the same letter as the first word in the row.

1. better	been	bag	doll
2. wish	wet	town	wind
3. face	if	family	fill
4. gold	song	ago	give
5. tan	tall	best	try
6. kind	keep	king	bake
7. color	doctor	come	our
8. might	miss	room	move
9. hand	hold	head	hole
10. bark	done	bite	door

Name _____

Standard: Initial Consonant Recognition

DIRECTIONS: Circle the words in each row that begin with the same letter as the first word in the row.

1. push	party	pot	bit
2. quiet	squirrel	queen	paint
3. you	yellow	yes	away
4. drink	drove	part	bone
5. seen	class	zoo	sister
6. never	name	nose	mean
7. light	until	lunch	long
8. class	cave	secret	cold
9. jump	into	just	sign
10. room	ready	rope	right

©2008 Plutarch Publications, Inc. PPI-1001

Name _____

Standard: Initial Consonant Recognition

DIRECTIONS: Circle the words in each row that begin with the same letter as the first word in the row.

1. miss	most	ham	making
2. yell	play	young	look
3. very	wave	have	visit
4. zoo	zoom	age	soon
5. guess	gone	girl	give
6. party	bag	drink	push
7. dinner	dance	band	duck
8. wet	was	vest	with
9. hear	never	help	house
10. nice	umbrella	many	note

©2008 Plutarch Publications, Inc. PPI-1001

Name _____   Standard: Final Consonant Recognition

DIRECTIONS: Circle the words in each row that end with the same letter that ends the first word in the row.

1. hat	pit	wait	toy
2. song	king	tiger	thing
3. plan	rain	again	soon
4. walk	talk	raking	rock
5. star	near	color	story
6. grow	water	snow	draw
7. miss	sky	faster	was
8. mad	found	feed	dinner
9. kitten	back	ran	kite
10. trip	picture	keep	help

©2008 Plutarch Publications, Inc. PPI-1001

Name _____ Standard: Final Consonant Recognition

DIRECTIONS: Circle the words in each row that end with the same letter that ends the first word in the row.

1. fell	hill	small	love
2. mean	note	sun	train
3. wood	were	cloud	sound
4. yell	fill	glass	school
5. hear	rabbit	dinner	turn
6. pot	first	light	place
7. sleep	park	step	top
8. drink	pick	keep	stuck
9. saw	was	snow	watch
10. room	mix	swim	mom

©2008 PLUTARCH PUBLICATIONS, Inc. PPI-1001

Name _____   Standard: Final Consonant Recognition

DIRECTIONS: Circle the words in each row that end with the same letter that ends the first word in the row.

1. cab	bat	bob	tub
2. box	fix	fox	flop
3. frog	grand	bag	pig
4. grass	bus	his	sun
5. them	hum	mail	bloom
6. low	new	wise	know
7. round	add	find	hop
8. boat	tag	seat	until
9. smell	color	full	below
10. ever	doctor	star	cart

©2008 Plutarch Publications, Inc. PPI -1001

Name _____   Standard: Word Recognition

DIRECTIONS:
Look at the word in each box. Circle the picture that the word names. The first one has been done for you.

letters	horse
	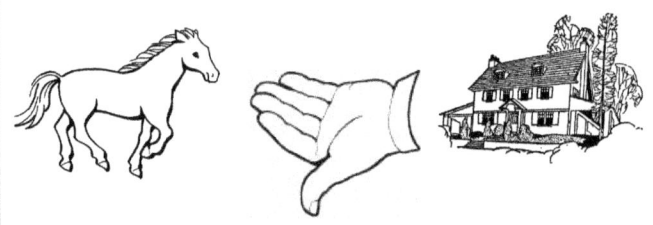
king	squirrel

nose	bus

doctor	table

Name _____   Standard: Word Recognition

DIRECTIONS:
Look at the word in each box. Circle the picture that the word names. The first one has been done for you.

watch 	teacher 
chair  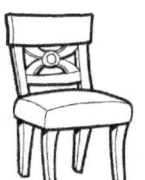 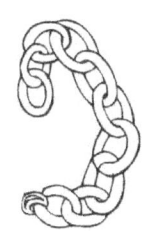	bike 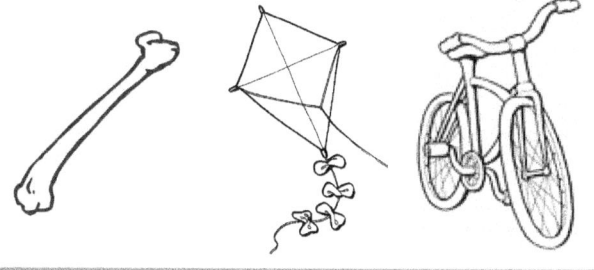
paint   	sheep 
money   	glass  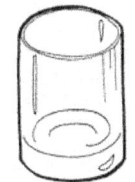 

Name _____   Standard: Word Recognition

DIRECTIONS:
Look at the word in each box. Circle the picture that the word names.
The first one has been done for you.

bell	umbrella

pony	tent
 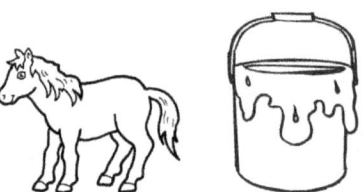	 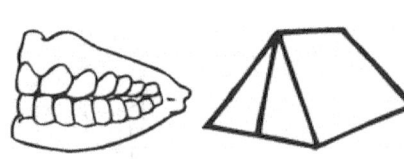
corn	nest
  	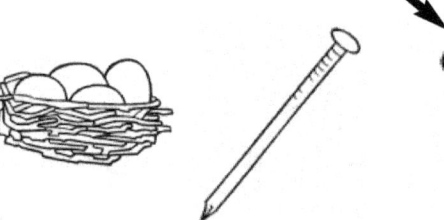
basket	five
  	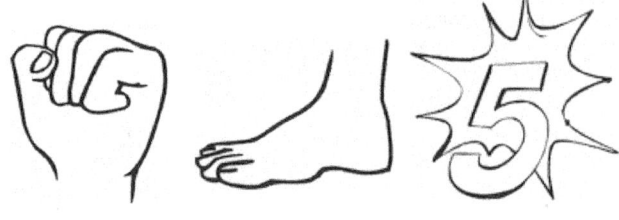

©2008 Plutarch Publications, Inc. PPI-1001

Name _____   Standard: Word Recognition

DIRECTIONS:
Underline the word that matches the picture.

again wood leg men		than train hungry inside	
because flower sang zoo		stand lunch star care	
fall chair fast clown		yell floor town head	
kind drink story glad		began grew bench most	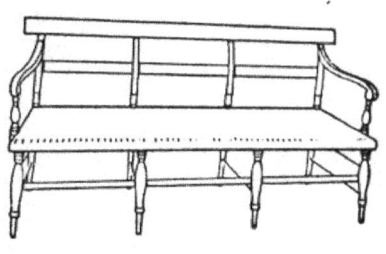

©2008 Plutarch Publications, Inc. PPI-1001

Name _____   Standard: Word Recognition

DIRECTIONS:
Underline the word that matches the picture.

apple ant any ate		cold clown cloud cave	
glass grass glad guess		letter light line lunch	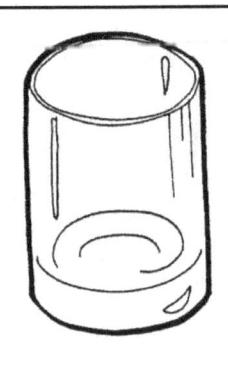
seat sheep sleep sister		nail nose note nine	
kick kind knee knock		tag tap tea toe	

©2008 Plutarch Publications, Inc. PPI-1001

Name _____   Standard: Words in Context

DIRECTIONS: Circle the word that matches the picture and completes each idea. Color the picture.

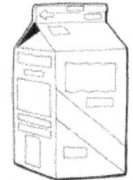
A glass of _____ is on the table.

milk   move

The bird is in the _____.

tire   tree

I can draw a _____.

pretty   picture

We will have an _____ for lunch.

apple   again

This is my _____ cake.

began   birthday

I _____ when I am happy.

smile   smell

©2008 Plutarch Publications, Inc. PPI-1001

Name _____   Standard: Words in Context

DIRECTIONS: Circle the word that matches the picture and completes each idea. Color the picture.

Open the door with this _____ .

kite   key   kitten

The _____ is green.

ball   bike   balloon

My mother has a _____ .

coat   cat   tiger

A mouse will eat the _____ .

chin   carrot   cheese

The cow is eating _____ .

green   grass   cloud

His car has a flat _____ .

tire   tree   tail

©2008 Plutarch Publications, Inc. PPI-1001

Name _____   Standard: Words in Context

DIRECTIONS: Circle the word that matches the picture and completes each idea. Color the picture.

We will play _____ .

      inside   outside

The _____ eats nuts.

      stone   squirrel

The bear _____ in a cave.

      lives   line

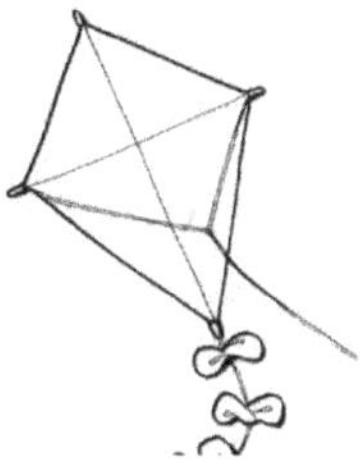

I like to fly my _____ .

      kite   kind

We took a ride on the _____ .

      train   trip

I have a new _____ .

      which   watch

©2008 Plutarch Publications, Inc. PPI -1001

Name _____   Standard: Words in Context

DIRECTIONS:
Underline the word that completes each idea. Color each picture.

 five black and white _____

      puppy   puppies

 a brown and white _____

      horse   horses

 two green and brown _____

      turtle   turtles

 a large cat and a small _____

      kitten   kittens

 four red and green _____

      ball   balls

 a blue and white _____

      bird   birds

©2008 Plutarch Publications, Inc. PPI-1001

Name _____   Standard: Words in Context

DIRECTIONS: Read the sentences in each box. Look at the picture. Underline the sentence that matches the picture.

<u>Mother is eating cake</u>.
It is a yellow cake.
She has a glass of milk.

It is a winter day.
I can see the snow.
I am wearing a coat.

We are sleeping.
It is a Halloween party!
I have a big balloon.

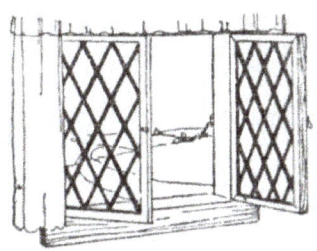

The wind is blowing.
The window is open.
The window is closed.

Cats are in the tree.
Squirrels are in the tree.
Squirrels are on the fence.

Name _____   Standard: Words in Context

DIRECTIONS: Read the sentences in each box. Look at the picture. Underline the sentence that matches the picture.

The girl is crying.
The baby is smiling.
The children are smiling.

The kitten is sleeping.
The kitten is in a box.
The kitten is under the table.

The flower needs water.
The flag needs water.
The flower is in the garden.

The milk is on the boy.
The mask is in a box.
The boy is wearing a mask.

Mother has a sandwich.
The man has a sandwich.
I am eating a sandwich.

Name _____ Standard: Rhyming

DIRECTIONS: Read the first word in each row. Circle the words in the row that rhyme with it.

1. ate	skate	late	date	ant
2. yell	you	sell	tell	bell
3. hop	hot	top	mop	pot
4. star	sat	far	car	can
5. cake	talk	take	make	care
6. bit	sit	fit	let	bat
7. night	note	right	sight	fight
8. sun	gun	fun	fan	run
9. store	tire	more	gone	for
10. gold	told	sold	good	fold

Name _____   Standard: Rhyming

DIRECTIONS: Read the first word in each row. Circle the words in the row that rhyme with it.

1. hat	mat	cat	fat	fan
2. bad	sad	mad	made	bat
3. box	ball	fox	ox	pot
4. cake	bake	rake	skate	take
5. tall	yell	wall	fall	ball
6. star	far	car	care	stay
7. hold	cold	hole	gold	bite
8. show	grow	wait	ever	know
9. kite	line	fight	white	light
10. wish	fish	wash	dish	next

Name _____ Standard: Synonyms

DIRECTIONS: Read the first word in each row. Circle the word in the row that means almost the same thing.

1. bunny	kitten	rabbit	boot
2. bake	bite	cook	pound
3. town	city	worker	light
4. pretty	around	beautiful	hungry
5. leave	rake	leg	go
6. hop	brother	stop	jump
7. fast	stuck	quick	ready
8. near	close	far	seat
9. start	begin	end	told
10. ship	zoo	boat	bone

©2008 Plutarch Publications, Inc. PPI-1001

Name _____   Standard: Synonyms

DIRECTIONS: Read the first word in each row. Circle the word in the row that means almost the same thing.

1. big	little	sorry	large
2. end	start	stop	our
3. mom	mother	father	girl
4. store	cave	shop	mean
5. nice	kind	draw	while
6. stone	stick	wind	rock
7. chair	seat	light	table
8. yell	tail	shout	quiet
9. glad	step	word	happy
10. road	grass	heard	street

Name _____   Standard: Synomyms

DIRECTIONS: Read the first word in each row. Circle the word in the row that means almost the same thing.

1. above	over	beside	below	in
2. indoor	outdoor	under	inside	room
3. invite	ask	agree	almost	able
4. final	start	last	first	only
5. afraid	angry	brave	scared	nice
6. smart	silly	happy	thin	wise
7. ship	truck	boat	shape	car
8. throw	work	game	toss	hit
9. large	little	small	big	tall
10. begin	start	awake	have	end

©2008 Plutarch Publications, Inc. PPI -1001

Name _____   Standard: Antonyms

DIRECTIONS: Read the first word in each row. Circle the word in the row that means the opposite.

1. on	top	off	gone
2. up	ran	only	down
3. play	story	work	yell
4. stop	far	bite	go
5. funny	sad	drink	girl
6. over	under	stick	give
7. fast	walk	slow	wet
8. tall	high	clean	short
9. winter	white	summer	plan
10. laugh	cry	smile	town

©2008 Plutarch Publications, Inc. PPI-1001

Name _____   Standard: Antonyms

DIRECTIONS: Read the first word in each row. Circle the word in the row that means the opposite.

1. lost	found	come	soon
2. good	best	feed	bad
3. walk	step	draw	run
4. go	come	sure	plant
5. keep	stay	take	yellow
6. last	only	clown	first
7. high	low	feel	sleep
8. hot	rain	cold	better
9. hello	sound	good-bye	part
10. big	long	grew	small

©2008 Plutarch Publications, Inc. PPI -1001

Name _____   Standard: Antonyms

DIRECTIONS: Read the first word in each row. Circle the word in the row that means the opposite.

1. loud	quiet	noisy	quit	lady
2. finish	over	begin	find	do
3. nearby	ever	close	moan	far
4. soft	smart	nice	hard	easy
5. whisper	talk	calm	camp	yell
6. shut	slam	open	door	fast
7. ugly	mean	pretty	good	nice
8. asleep	awake	upset	down	shy
9. west	wake	wide	north	east
10. women	people	men	lady	boy

Name _____   Standard: Riddles

DIRECTIONS: Read the riddle in each box. Underline the word that answers each riddle.

I am baked in the oven. I am for a birthday. You can eat me. What am I?	a kite a cake a kitten
I am an animal. I live in a barn. I say moo. What am I?	a horse an ant a cow
I am white and cold. I fall on winter days. You can walk on me. What am I?	candy snow rain
We are alive. We can eat and grow. We have faces and eyes. What are we?	children flowers stones
I am a toy. I have two tires. You can ride me. What am I?	a boat a train a bike

©2008 Plutarch Publications, Inc. PPI-1001

Name _____   Standard: Riddles

DIRECTIONS: Read the riddle in each box. Underline the word that answers each riddle.

I have hands. I have a face. You use me to tell time. What am I?	a kitten a watch a dinner
I push kites high in the sky. I blow on you. You can not see me. What am I?	the sun a cloud the wind
I am something to eat. I am good for you. You eat me in the morning. What am I?	breakfast lunch dinner
I am in your house. I am in your school. You can sit on me. What am I?	a store a horse a chair
I am a boy. I am part of your family. I am not your father. Who am I?	mother brother sister

Name _____   Standard: Riddles

DIRECTIONS: Read the riddle in each box. Underline the word that answers each riddle.

I am something you can do. I am done at night. I am done in bed. What am I?	sleep run give
I am in your house. I am not alive. You can watch me. What am I?	a baby a window a TV
I am in the back. Many animals have me. Sometimes I can wag. What am I?	a tail a nose a coat
I am green. I live outside in your yard. You walk and play on me. What am I?	a frog a car grass
I am a white light. I am up in the sky. You can only see me at night. What am I?	the sun a star a bird

Name _____   Standard: Following Directions

DIRECTIONS: Read the sentences then do what they say.

Here are three balls.
Color the middle one blue.
Draw an X on the first one.
Color the last one green.
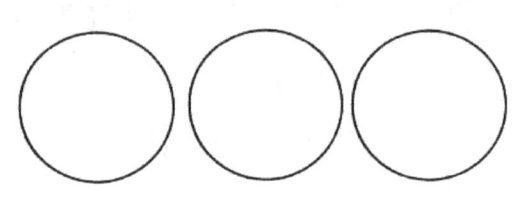

Here are two cars.
Circle the big car.
Color the little car red.
Color the big car yellow.

Here are four birds.
Draw an X on the first bird.
Circle the last bird.
Put a 2 on the second bird.

Here are two boxes.
Draw another box.
Color the first box orange.
Circle the box you drew.
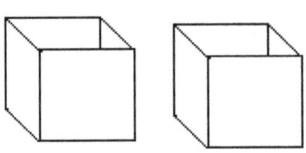

Here is a girl.
Draw a smile on the girl.
Color her hair brown.
Put an X next to the girl.

©2008 Plutarch Publications, Inc. PPI-1001

Name _____   Standard: Following Directions

DIRECTIONS: Read the sentences then do what they say.

Here are two cats and a dog.
Circle the dog.
Draw a line under the little cat.
Color the big cat black.

Here is a big fish.
Draw three little fish behind it.
Color all the little fish purple.
Put an X on the big fish.

Here are four socks.
Circle the third sock.
Color the first sock blue.
Put a box around the last sock.
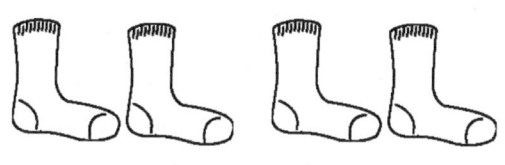

Here are three eggs.
Color the middle egg red.
Circle the last egg.
Put an X on the first egg.
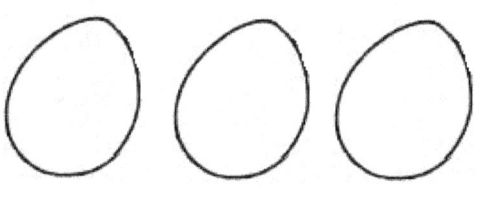

Here is a box.
Draw a ball next to the box.
Color the star yellow.
Color the ball brown.
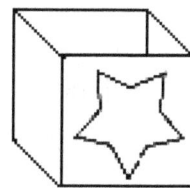

Name ──────────────   Standard: Following Directions

DIRECTIONS: Read the sentences then do what they say.

Here are two snowmen.
Draw a hat on the first snowman.
Put three buttons on the second snowman.
Give the first snowman a scarf.

Here are four apples.
Put a leaf on the third apple.
Color the first apple red.
Draw a circle around the last apple.
Draw a box around the second apple.

Here is one hat.
Draw a line under the hat.
Color the hat yellow and green.
Put an X above the hat.
Put an O next to the hat.

Here are two children.
Draw a circle around the girl.
Put a line under the boy.
Color the boy's pants blue.
Color the girl's hair brown.

Here are two books.
Write the letter "A" on the big book. Color the little book orange.
Put an X over the small book.
Circle the large book.
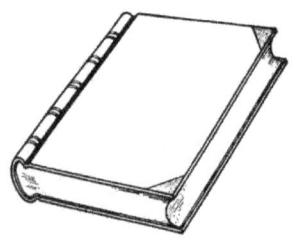

©2008 Plutarch Publications, Inc. PPI -1001

Name _____   Standard: Synonyms

DIRECTIONS: Underline the words in each row that mean almost the same thing as the underlined word in each sentence.

1.	It is a sunny day with no clouds.	bright	dark
2.	She lives in a large town.	house	city
3.	He was lost in the woods.	grass	forest
4.	Help! The water is over my head.	above	below
5.	Put a lid on the jar.	cover	corner
6.	Paste the paper together.	glass	glue
7.	Don't get lost! Follow the trail.	path	trunk
8.	Wise people know many things!	young	smart
9.	The nest was made of twigs.	sticks	stones
10.	Plants need soil to grow.	dirt	rake
11.	Carry the books in a sack.	bag	pencil
12.	I like to swim in the ocean.	street	sea
13.	Wear a coat. It is cool outside.	cold	warm
14.	Please shut the door.	open	close
15.	We will nap after lunch.	sleep	eat

©2008 Plutarch Publications, Inc. PPI-1001

Name _____   Standard: Synonyms

DIRECTIONS: Underline the words in each row that mean almost the same thing as the underlined word in each sentence.

1. The flower is <u>pretty</u>.	beautiful	old	yellow
2. We <u>began</u> the party.	ended	see	started
3. Do not <u>yell</u> at her!	without	shout	any
4. Please sit in this <u>chair</u>.	seat	those	wet
5. Pat runs <u>quickly</u>.	slowly	tall	fast
6. John is <u>kind</u> to me.	secret	nice	mean
7. Don't throw that <u>rock</u>!	stone	drink	money
8. Did mother <u>cook</u> that?	together	bake	buy
9. The <u>rabbit</u> is hopping.	bunny	right	horse
10. The <u>boat</u> is out to sea.	brother	ship	train
11. Stand <u>close</u> to me.	away	push	near
12. Cross the <u>street</u> now.	sister	room	road
13. <u>Father</u> is a good man.	flower	dad	boy
14. I am <u>happy</u> to help.	glad	sad	angry
15. That <u>woman</u> is tall.	worker	girl	lady

©2008 Plutarch Publications, Inc. PPI-1001

Name _____   Standard: Words in Context

DIRECTIONS: Circle the word that completes each sentence. Write the word in the blank.

1. Mother _____ at the school.	work works
2. Peter _____ six cats.	have has
3. Tasha will _____ the glass.	fill fell
4. Jim is home _____.	alone along
5. I am taller _____ you.	that than
6. I need a new _____ for my bike.	try tire
7. The _____ likes to bark.	sheep puppy
8. Father _____ yesterday.	drove drive
9. She did it by _____.	myself herself
10. Set the _____ for dinner.	table track
11. Mom asked me to be _____.	quiet noise
12. You can run _____ than me.	fast faster
13. It is time to _____ for school.	love leave
14. Did the party already _____?	begin began
15. I _____ cookies!	small smell

©2008 PLUTARCH PUBLICATIONS, INC. PPI-1001

Name _____   Standard: Words in Context

DIRECTIONS: Circle the word that completes each sentence. Write the word in the blank.

1. She _____ playing games.	was were
2. Wash your hands to _____ them.	clean class
3. I will read a _____ to you.	stone story
4. The _____ is blowing hard!	wish wind
5. I need a _____ of water.	drink drove
6. I _____ to do my best.	tried tries
7. We had a _____ time today!	grew great
8. I will _____ how many.	guess glass
9. My _____ is older than me.	sound sister
10. I am _____ in the mud.	stuck stand
11. You have a nice _____.	smells smile
12. _____ apples are ready to eat.	Those This
13. _____ piece of cake is mine?	Which Word
14. It is a dark _____.	night tonight
15. You may _____ the book.	keeps keep

Name _____   Standard: Words in Context

DIRECTIONS: Circle the word that completes each sentence. Write the word in the blank.

1. That is a _____ idea!	super	supper
2. A duck can _____ .	quick	quack
3. My mother _____ a letter.	sent	seat
4. I will _____ the cat.	fed	feed
5. The soup is in a _____ .	bow	bowl
6. There is a _____ in the fence.	gate	grab
7. Two cows are in the _____ .	bare	barn
8. The birds are in their _____ .	nest	neck
9. I can eat an _____ .	egg	edge
10. That key will open the _____ .	lock	luck
11. Please _____ your hands!	wife	wash
12. The bell will _____ soon.	rang	ring
13. The baby is very _____ .	tiny	toss
14. Will you _____ your candy?	sharp	share
15. The cake is in the _____ .	oven	order

©2008 Plutarch Publications, Inc. PPI-1001

Name _____   Standard: Answer Questions

DIRECTIONS: Read each question. Choose a word from the word box to help answer the question. Write your answer.

1. What can we read? | rope   paint   book
_____

2. What smells good? | kite   cake   wish
_____

3. What do people eat? | food   hungry   fine
_____

4. What falls from a cloud? | grass   rain   than
_____

5. What can we drink? | light   water   feed
_____

6. Where can we swim? | chair   secret   lake
_____

7. What is in the night sky? | star   stick   sun
_____

Name _____   Standard: Answer Questions

DIRECTIONS: Read each question. Choose a word from the word box to help answer the question. Write your answer.

1. What do you play with?	inside rooms toys
	_____

2. What can grow?	flowers bikes steps
	_____

3. What lives in a nest?	dog nose bird
	_____

4. What feels very cold?	snow tiger cake
	_____

5. What is a part of your body?	plan head tire
	_____

6. What is a meal we eat?	lunch table cook
	_____

7. Where do we see animals?	dance better zoo
	_____

Name _____   Standard: Narrative Stories

DIRECTIONS: Read the story then answer the questions.

My Pet

I have a pet rabbit. His name is Puff. He has a fluffy tail and long ears. I take him for a walk every day. We play together. He is a nice pet.

1. What is the name of this story?

   _____

2. What kind of animal is my pet?

   _____

3. What is the name of my pet?

   _____

4. What two things does Puff have?

   _____

5. Where do I take Puff every day?

   _____

6. What can Puff and I do together?

   _____

7. What kind of pet would you like to have?

   _____

Name —————————————————— Standard: Narrative Stories

DIRECTIONS: Read the story then answer the questions.

Playing Together

Matt and Pat played together today. They hit a ball with a bat. They rode their bikes and played with toys in the sandbox. They were tired by dinner time.

1. What is the name of this story?

   _____

2. Who played together?

   _____

3. What did they use to hit the ball?

   _____

4. What did Matt and Pat ride?

   _____

5. Where did they play with their toys?

   _____

6. How did Matt and Pat feel by dinner time?

   _____

7. What do you like to play with your friends?

   _____

Name _____   Standard: Narrative Stories

DIRECTIONS: Read the story then answer the questions.

At the Zoo

 Our zoo is very nice. The tigers and lions roar. The seals swim and do tricks. Monkeys swing from trees and make faces at us. They make us laugh!

1. What is the name of this story?

   _____

2. Which animals can roar?

   _____

3. Which animals do tricks?

   _____

4. What two things can the seals do?

   _____

5. Which animals swing in the trees?

   _____

6. Which animals make us laugh?

   _____

7. What is your favorite animal at the zoo?

   _____

Name _____   Standard: Narrative Stories

DIRECTIONS: Read the story then answer the questions.

My Birthday

Today is my birthday. I am six years old! My friends will come to my party. We will play games and eat cake. I will make a wish and blow out the candles. It will be fun.

1. What is the name of this story?
   _____

2. Why am I having a party today?
   _____

3. How old am I today?
   _____

4. Who will come to my party?
   _____

5. What will we do at the party?
   _____

6. When will I make a wish?
   _____

7. What will you wish for on your birthday?
   _____

©2008 Plutarch Publications, Inc. PPI -1001

Name _____ Standard: Narrative Stories

DIRECTIONS: Read the story then answer the questions.

Baby Sister

Sue has a new baby sister named Ann. Sue helps Mother with Ann. Sue holds the baby and helps feed her, too. Mother says that Sue is a good big sister for baby Ann.

1. What is the name of this story?
   _____

2. Who has a new baby sister?
   _____

3. What is the baby's name?
   _____

4. Who does Sue help?
   _____

5. What two things does Sue do to help?
   _____

6. What does Mother say about Sue?
   _____

7. How would you help with a new baby?
   _____

Name _____   Standard: Narrative Stories

DIRECTIONS: Read the poem then answer the questions.

Wake Up!
Baby sister sitting there,
Sleeping in your high chair.
What made you so tired today?
Please wake up. I want to play!

1. What is this poem about?

   _____

2. Who is sleeping?

   _____

3. Why is the baby sleeping?

   _____

4. How long has the baby been asleep?

   _____

5. Why does this person want the baby to wake up?

   _____

6. Is the person speaking a boy or a girl?

   _____

7. What game might you play with a baby?

   _____

©2008 Plutarch Publications, Inc. PPI -1001

Name _____   Standard: Narrative Stories

DIRECTIONS: Read the poem then answer the questions.

A Bus Ride

Today Grandma and I took a bus to the mall. We waited at the bus stop and soon a big blue bus pulled up. I helped Grandma go up the steps and we sat in the seat behind the driver. There were many people on the bus. It was a fun ride!

1. What is the title of this story?

   _____

2. Where were Grandma and I going?

   _____

3. What color was the bus?

   _____

4. In which seat did Grandma and I sit?

   _____

5. Where did we wait for the bus?

   _____

6. How did I help Grandma?

   _____

7. Where would you like to go on a bus?

   _____

Name _____ Standard: Narrative Stories

DIRECTIONS: Read the story then answer the questions.

Friends

Jeff is my best friend. We are both boys. Jeff is tall and I am short. I have brown eyes but Jeff's eyes are blue. I like to run but Jeff likes to climb trees. We are very different, but we have lots of fun together.

1. What is the title of this story?

   _____

2. How are Jeff and I alike?

   _____

3. Who is taller, Jeff or me?

   _____

4. What color are my eyes?

   _____

5. Who likes to climb trees?

   _____

6. Which boy has a dog for a pet?

   _____

7. Who is your best friend?

   _____

Name _____   Standard: Narrative Stories

DIRECTIONS: Read the story then answer the questions.

Helping the Family

Jean has a large family. There are many things that need to be done. Jean helps by making her bed every morning before school. She sets the table for dinner every night. She reads to her little brother, too. Jean helps her family by doing her jobs well.

1. What is the title of this story?

   _____

2. Who is this story about?

   _____

3. How many jobs does Jean have?

   _____

4. What job does Jean do in the morning?

   _____

5. What is Jean's job at dinner time?

   _____

6. How many people are in Jean's family?

   _____

7. How do you think Jean's jobs help her family?

   _____

Name _____   Standard: Nonfictional Stories

DIRECTIONS: Read the story then answer the questions.

Plants

Plants are living things. They have roots, stems, and leaves. The stem is the part that holds up the plant. The roots and leaves gather rain and sun to make food. Many of the foods we eat come from plants.

1. What is this story about?

   _____

2. How many parts does a plant have?

   _____

3. What are the three parts of a plant?

   _____

4. How do the roots and leaves help the plant?

   _____

5. Which part holds up the plant?

   _____

6. Are plants alive?

   _____

7. Name a food that comes from a plant.

   _____

Name _____ Standard: Nonfictional Stories

DIRECTIONS: Read the story then answer the questions.

Matter

Matter is anything that has weight and takes up space. Matter can be solid like your desk, liquid like water, or gas like the air. Everything around us is matter. We are matter, too!

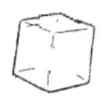 solid

 liquid

 gas

1. What is the topic of this story?

   _____

2. What is matter?

   _____

3. Name the three types of matter.

   _____

4. What kind of matter is milk?

   _____

5. What kind of matter is a box?

   _____

6. Is a book solid, liquid, or gas matter?

   _____

7. Water is a liquid. What kind of matter is ice?

   _____

©2008 Plutarch Publications, Inc. PPI -1001

Name _____   Standard: Nonfictional Stories

DIRECTIONS: Read the story then answer the questions.

Senses

People smell with noses, hear with ears, taste with tongues, feel with skin, and see with eyes. These five things are called senses and they help us learn about our world.

- smell
- hear
- taste
- feel
- see

1. What is the topic of this story?

   _____

2. How many senses do people have?

   _____

3. Which sense uses our eyes?

   _____

4. Which part of our body helps us hear?

   _____

5. Which part of our body helps us smell?

   _____

6. Why do we need senses?

   _____

7. Which sense do you like to use the most?

   _____

Name _____ Standard: Nonfictional Stories

DIRECTIONS: Read the story then answer the questions.

The Night Sky

The night sky is full of stars. Stars are balls of burning gases like our Sun, but they are very far away. The moon is in our night sky, too. The moon is a large rock that circles the Earth. It reflects light from our Sun.

1. What is the topic of this story?

   _____

2. Name two things we can see in our night sky.

   _____

3. What are stars?

   _____

4. What is the moon?

   _____

5. Do the stars or the moon circle the Earth?

   _____

6. Why does the moon shine?

   _____

7. What do you like best in the night sky?

   _____

Name _____   Standard: Nonfictional Stories

DIRECTIONS: Read the story then answer the questions.

Weather

Is the sun out or is it cloudy? Is it raining or snowing? Is it hot or cold outside? These things make up our weather. Weather helps plants grow and gives animals water. People need weather to keep us warm or cool and to grow food.

1. What is the topic of this story?

   _____

2. How does weather help people?

   _____

3. How does weather help plants?

   _____

4. Name three types of weather.

   _____

5. How does the rain help animals?

   _____

6. Why do we need weather?

   _____

7. What is your favorite kind of weather?

   _____

Name _____   Standard: Reading Maps

DIRECTIONS: Use the map to answer the questions.

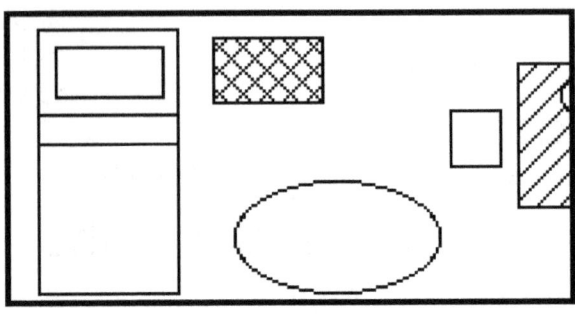

A Map of My Bedroom

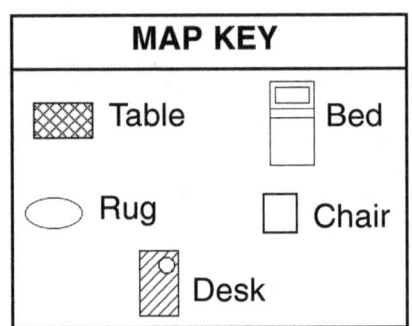

1. What does this map show?

   _____

2. How many chairs are in my room?

   _____

3. What is in front of my desk?

   _____

4. What is next to my bed near the pillow?

   _____

5. Is the rug nearer the head or the foot of my bed?

   _____

6. Where is the door to my room?

   _____

7. How many rugs are in my room?

   _____

Name _____   Standard: Reading Maps

DIRECTIONS: Use the map to answer the questions.

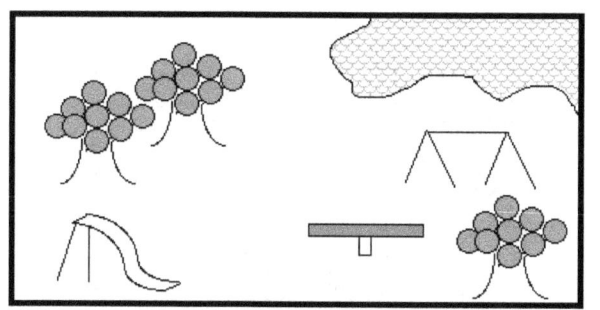
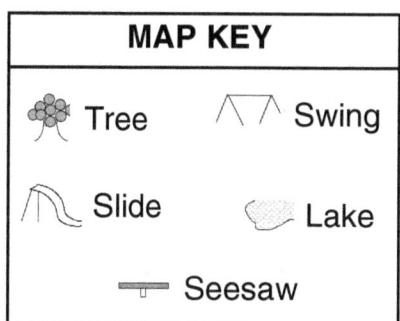

A Map of the Park

1. What does this map show?

   _____

2. How many trees are in the park?

   _____

3. What is closer to the lake, a tree or the slide?

   _____

4. What two things are near the seesaw?

   _____

5. What two things are just above the slide?

   _____

6. How many lakes are shown on this map?

   _____

7. How many children play in the park each day?

   _____

©2008 Plutarch Publications, Inc. PPI -1001

ANSWER KEYS: 6, 7, 8, 9

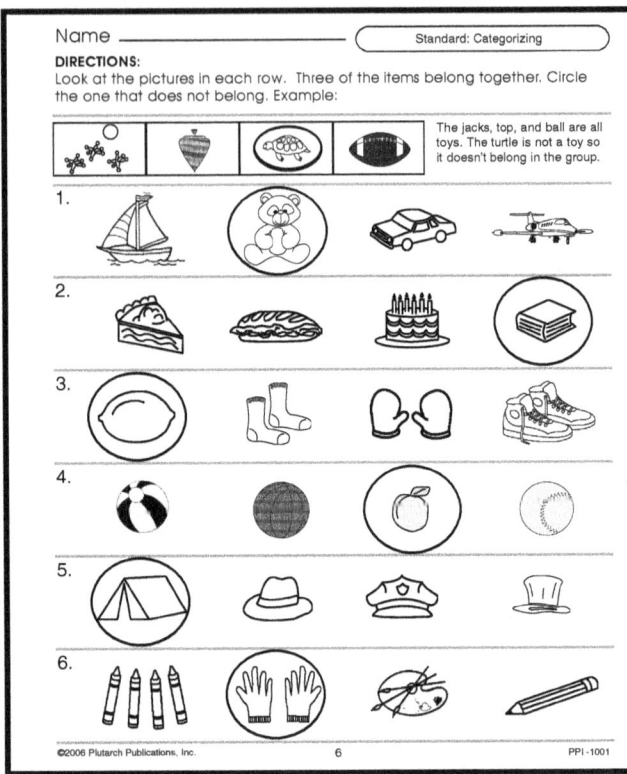

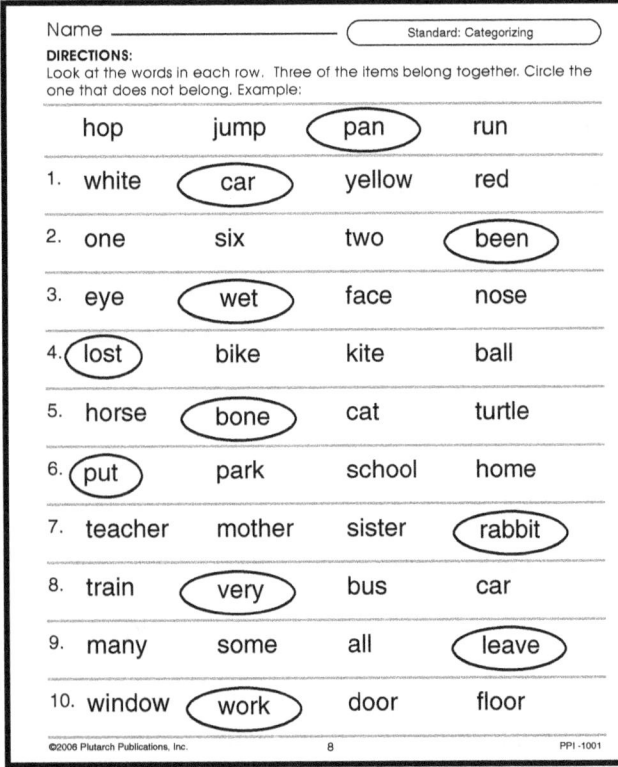
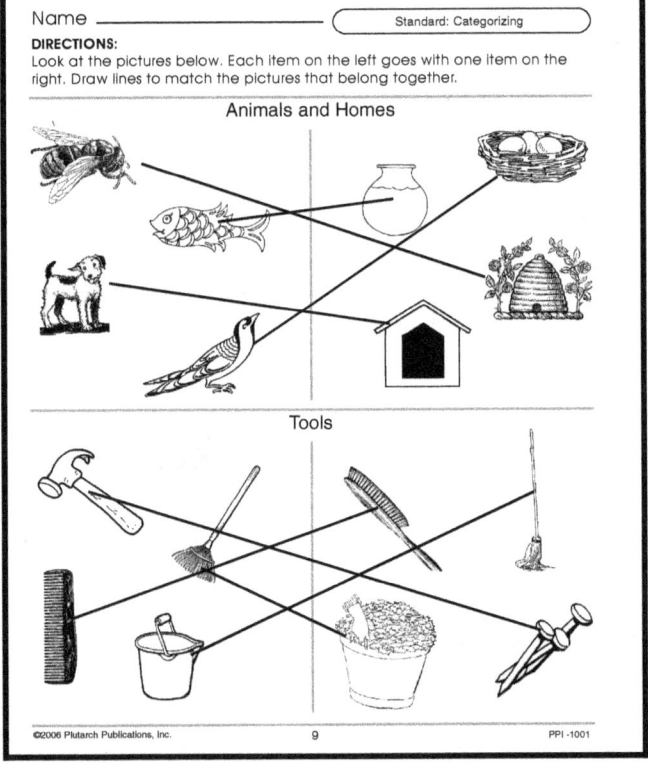

ANSWER KEYS: 10, 11, 12, 13

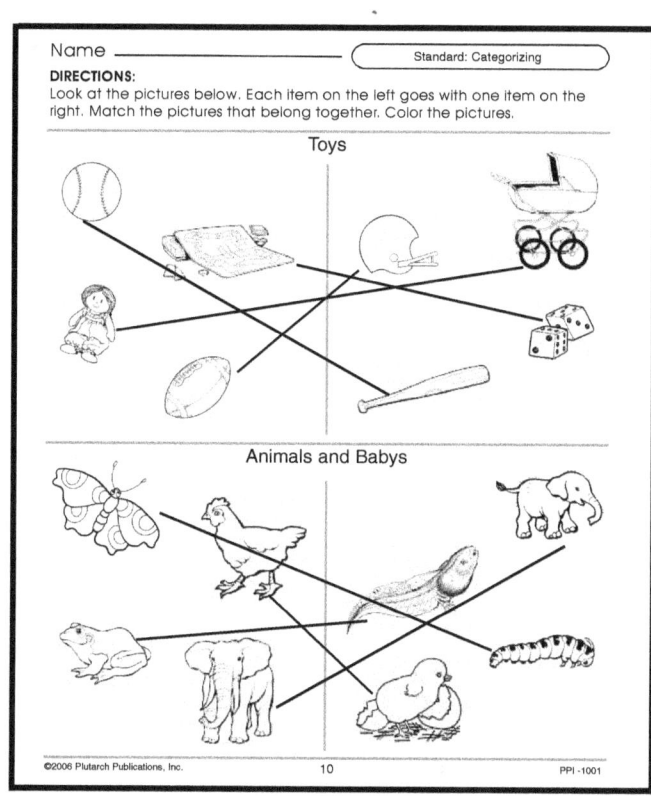

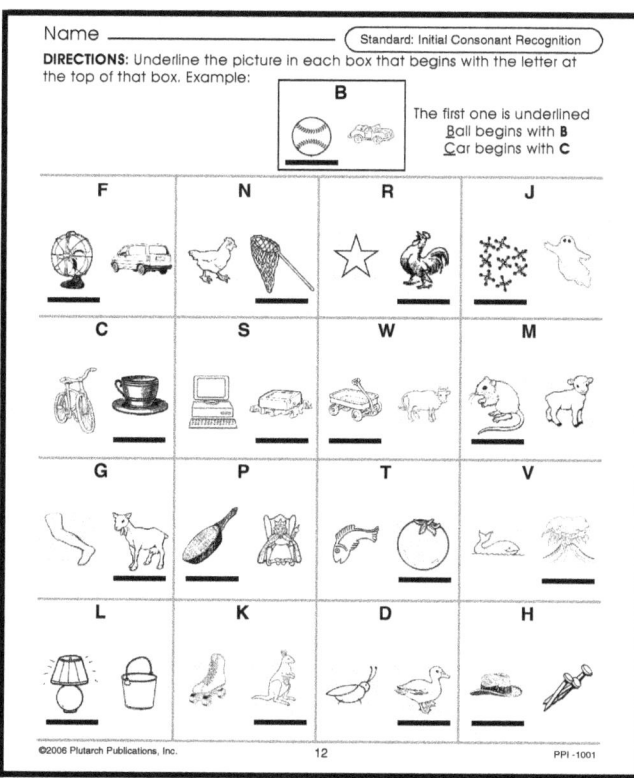

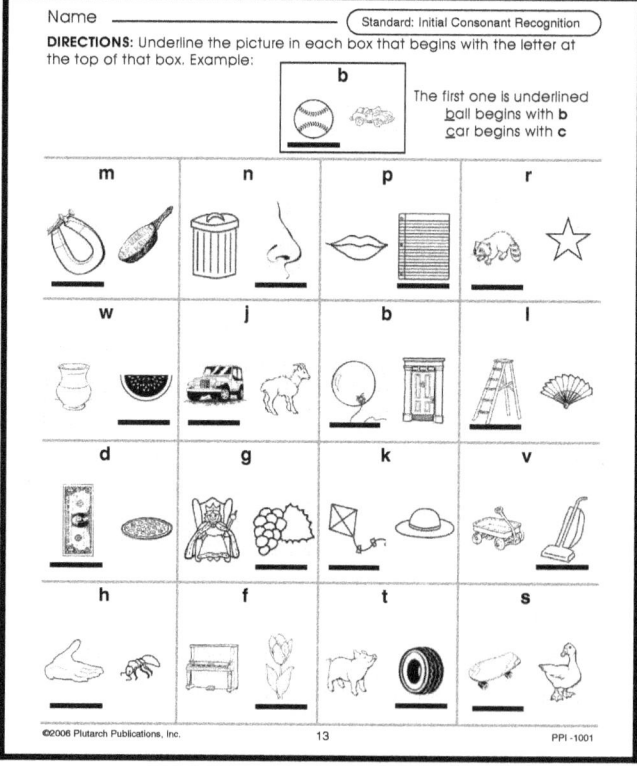

ANSWER KEYS: 14, 15, 16, 17

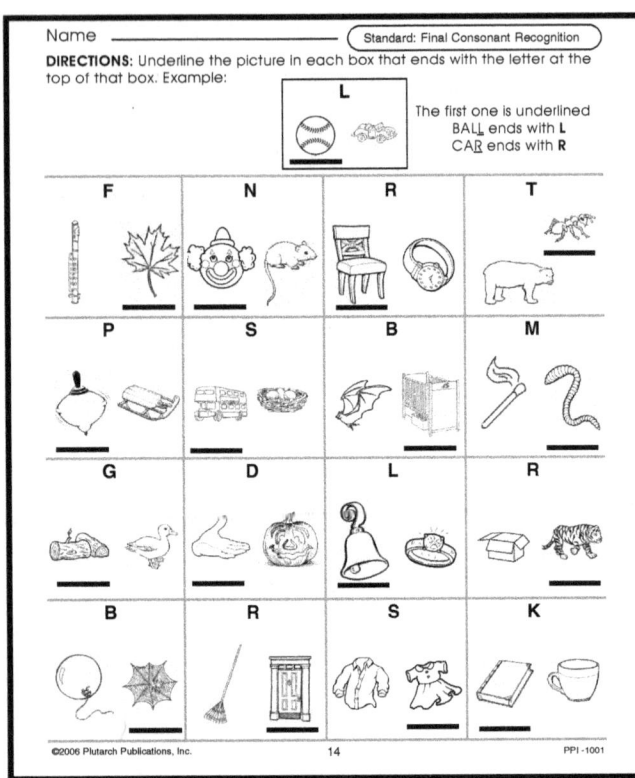

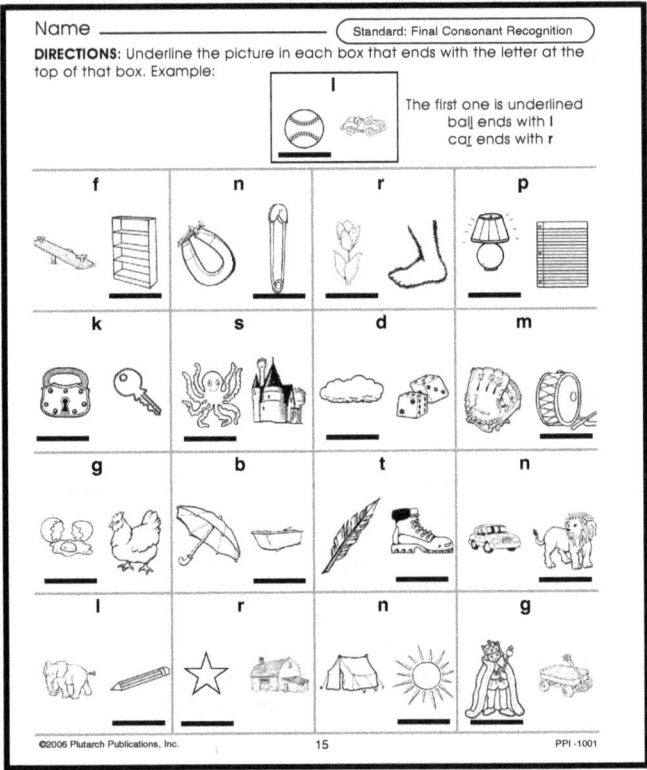

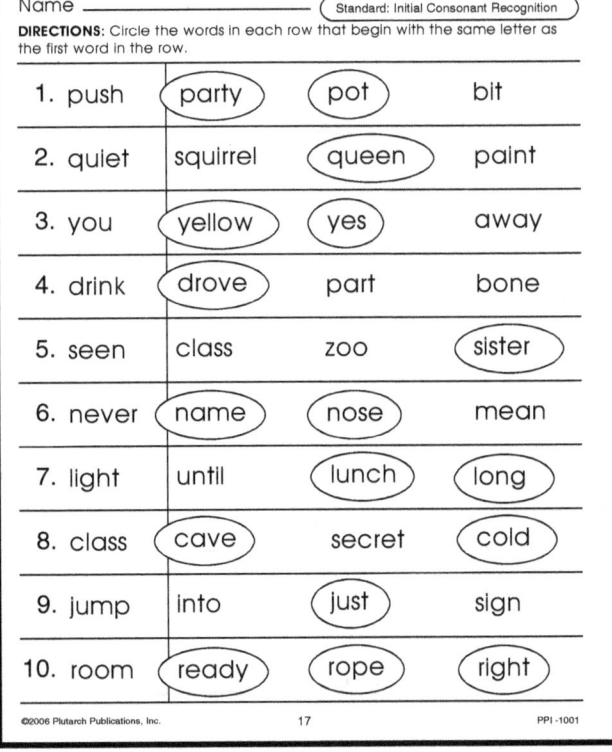

ANSWER KEYS: 18, 19, 20, 21

Name _____   Standard: Initial Consonant Recognition

DIRECTIONS: Circle the words in each row that begin with the same letter as the first word in the row.

1. miss	(most)	ham	(making)
2. yell	play	(young)	look
3. very	wave	have	(visit)
4. zoo	(zoom)	age	soon
5. guess	(gone)	(girl)	(give)
6. party	bag	drink	(push)
7. dinner	(dance)	band	(duck)
8. wet	(was)	vest	(with)
9. hear	never	(help)	(house)
10. nice	umbrella	many	(note)

18

Name _____   Standard: Final Consonant Recognition

DIRECTIONS: Circle the words in each row that end with the same letter that ends the first word in the row.

1. hat	(pit)	(wait)	toy
2. song	(king)	tiger	(thing)
3. plan	(rain)	(again)	(soon)
4. walk	(talk)	raking	(rock)
5. star	(near)	(color)	story
6. grow	water	(snow)	(draw)
7. miss	sky	faster	(was)
8. mad	(found)	(feed)	dinner
9. kitten	back	(ran)	kite
10. trip	picture	(keep)	(help)

19

Name _____   Standard: Final Consonant Recognition

DIRECTIONS: Circle the words in each row that end with the same letter that ends the first word in the row.

1. fell	(hill)	(small)	love
2. mean	note	(sun)	(train)
3. wood	were	(cloud)	(sound)
4. yell	(fill)	glass	(school)
5. hear	rabbit	(dinner)	turn
6. pot	(first)	(light)	place
7. sleep	park	(step)	(top)
8. drink	(pick)	keep	(stuck)
9. saw	was	(snow)	watch
10. room	mix	(swim)	(mom)

20

Name _____   Standard: Final Consonant Recognition

DIRECTIONS: Circle the words in each row that end with the same letter that ends the first word in the row.

1. cab	bat	(bob)	(tub)
2. box	(fix)	(fox)	flop
3. frog	grand	(bag)	(pig)
4. grass	(bus)	(his)	sun
5. them	(hum)	mail	(bloom)
6. low	(new)	wise	(know)
7. round	(add)	(find)	hop
8. boat	tag	(seat)	until
9. smell	color	(full)	below
10. ever	(doctor)	(star)	cart

21

ANSWER KEYS: 22, 23, 24, 25

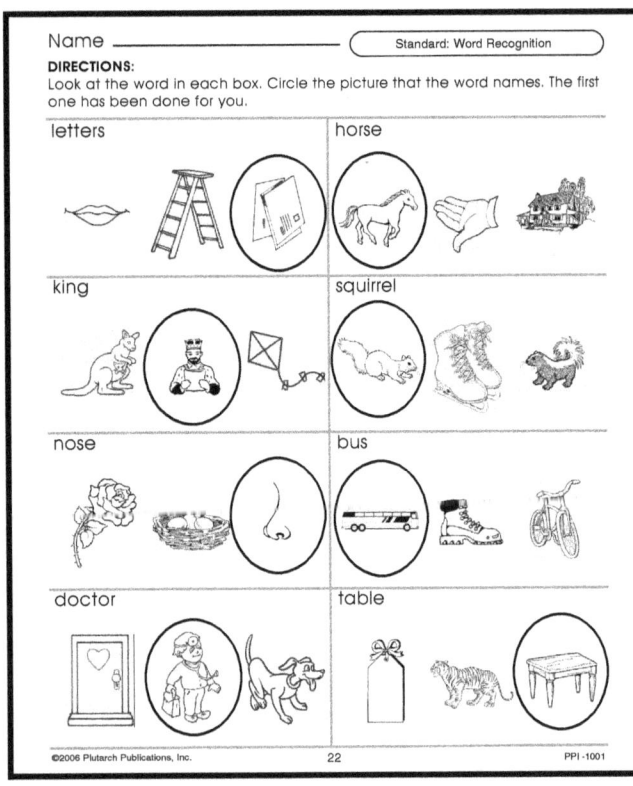
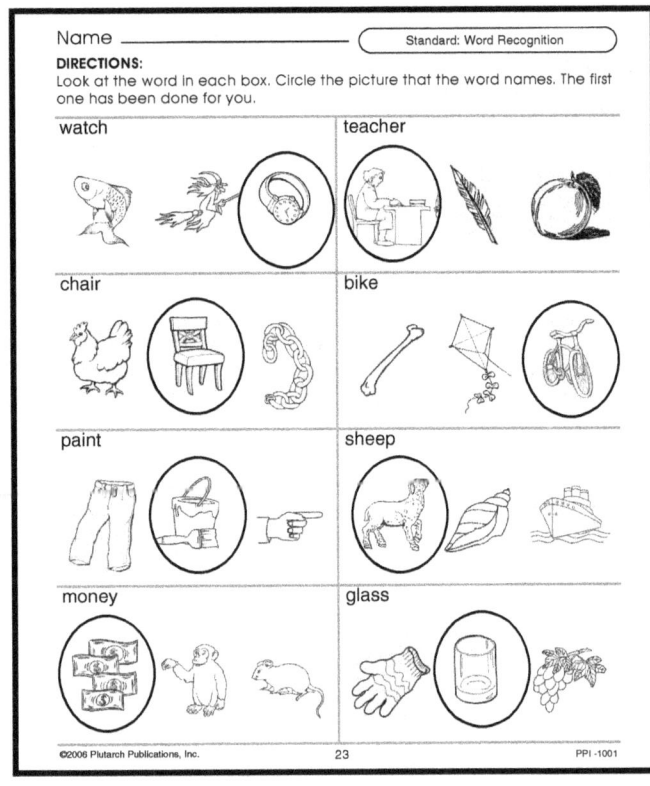
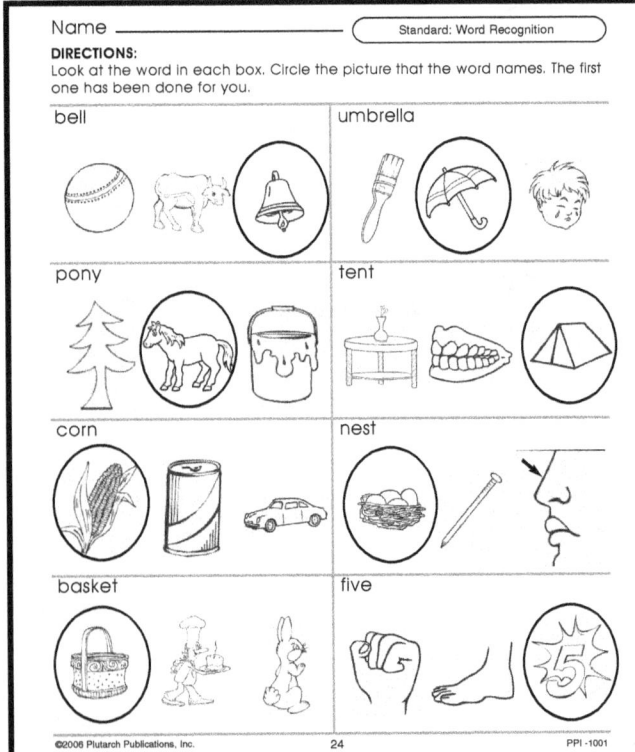

ANSWER KEYS: 26, 27, 28, 29

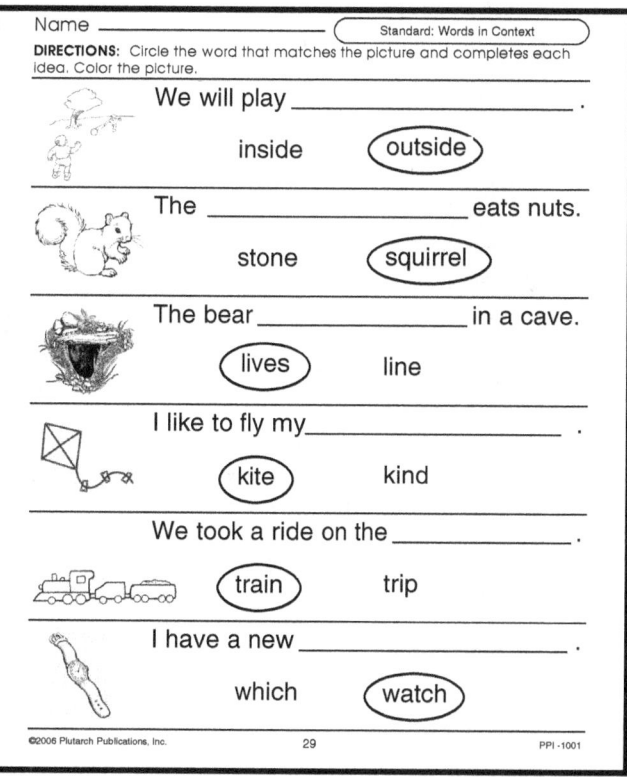

ANSWER KEYS: 30, 31, 32, 33

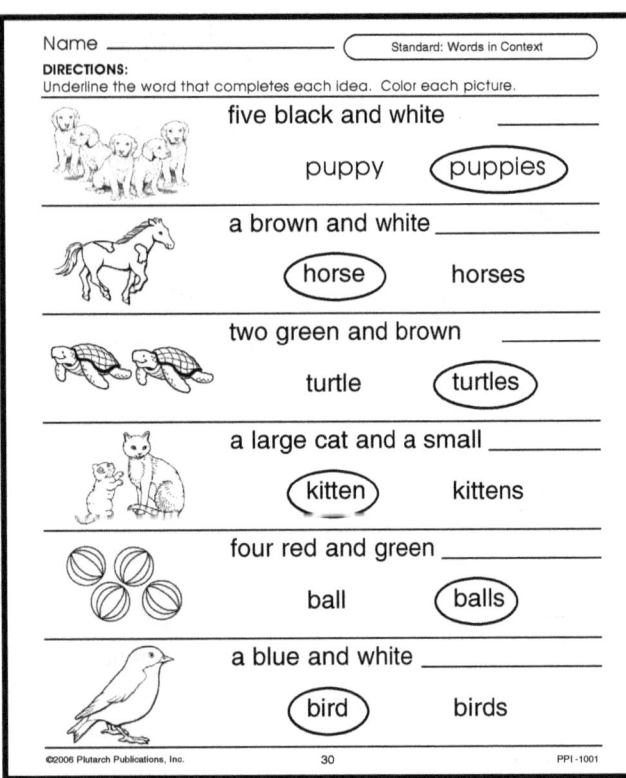

ANSWER KEYS: 34, 35, 36, 37

Name _____ Standard: Rhyming
DIRECTIONS: Read the first word in each row. Circle the words in the row that rhyme with it.

1. hat	(mat)	(cat)	(fat)	fan
2. bad	(sad)	(mad)	made	bat
3. box	ball	(fox)	(ox)	pot
4. cake	(bake)	(rake)	skate	(take)
5. tall	yell	(wall)	(fall)	(ball)
6. star	(far)	(car)	care	stay
7. hold	(cold)	hole	(gold)	bite
8. show	(grow)	wait	ever	(know)
9. kite	line	(fight)	(white)	(light)
10. wish	(fish)	wash	(dish)	next

Name _____ Standard: Synonyms
DIRECTIONS: Read the first word in each row. Circle the word in the row that means almost the same thing.

1. bunny	kitten	(rabbit)	boot	
2. bake	bite	(cook)	pound	
3. town	(city)	worker	light	
4. pretty	around	(beautiful)	hungry	
5. leave	rake	leg	(go)	
6. hop	brother	stop	(jump)	
7. fast	stuck	(quick)	ready	
8. near	(close)	far	seat	
9. start	(begin)	end	told	
10. ship	zoo	(boat)	bone	

Name _____ Standard: Synonyms
DIRECTIONS: Read the first word in each row. Circle the word in the row that means almost the same thing.

1. big	little	sorry	(large)	
2. end	start	(stop)	our	
3. mom	(mother)	father	girl	
4. store	cave	(shop)	mean	
5. nice	(kind)	draw	while	
6. stone	stick	wind	(rock)	
7. chair	(seat)	light	table	
8. yell	tail	(shout)	quiet	
9. glad	step	word	(happy)	
10. road	grass	heard	(street)	

Name _____ Standard: Synonyms
DIRECTIONS: Read the first word in each row. Circle the word in the row that means almost the same thing.

1. above	(over)	beside	below	in
2. indoor	outdoor	under	(inside)	room
3. invite	(ask)	agree	almost	able
4. final	start	(last)	first	only
5. afraid	angry	brave	(scared)	nice
6. smart	silly	happy	thin	(wise)
7. ship	truck	(boat)	shape	car
8. throw	work	game	(toss)	hit
9. large	little	small	(big)	tall
10. begin	(start)	awake	have	end

ANSWER KEYS: 38, 39, 40, 41

Worksheet 38 — Standard: Antonyms

DIRECTIONS: Read the first word in each row. Circle the word in the row that means the opposite.

1. on — top — (off) — gone
2. up — ran — only — (down)
3. play — story — (work) — yell
4. stop — far — bite — (go)
5. funny — (sad) — drink — girl
6. over — (under) — stick — give
7. fast — walk — (slow) — wet
8. tall — high — clean — (short)
9. winter — white — (summer) — plan
10. laugh — (cry) — smile — town

Worksheet 39 — Standard: Antonyms

DIRECTIONS: Read the first word in each row. Circle the word in the row that means the opposite.

1. lost — (found) — come — soon
2. good — best — feed — (bad)
3. walk — step — draw — (run)
4. go — (come) — sure — plant
5. keep — stay — (take) — yellow
6. last — only — clown — (first)
7. high — (low) — feel — sleep
8. hot — rain — (cold) — better
9. hello — sound — (good-bye) — part
10. big — long — grew — (small)

Worksheet 40 — Standard: Antonyms

DIRECTIONS: Read the first word in each row. Circle the word in the row that means the opposite.

1. loud — (quiet) — noisy — quit — lady
2. finish — over — (begin) — find — do
3. nearby — ever — close — moan — (far)
4. soft — smart — nice — (hard) — easy
5. whisper — talk — calm — camp — (yell)
6. shut — slam — (open) — door — fast
7. ugly — mean — (pretty) — good — nice
8. asleep — (awake) — upset — down — shy
9. west — wake — wide — north — (east)
10. women — people — (men) — lady — boy

Worksheet 41 — Standard: Riddles

DIRECTIONS: Read the riddle in each box. Underline the word that answers each riddle.

I am baked in the oven.
I am for a birthday.
You can eat me.
What am I?
- a kite
- <u>a cake</u>
- a kitten

I am an animal.
I live in a barn.
I say moo.
What am I?
- a horse
- an ant
- <u>a cow</u>

I am white and cold.
I fall on winter days.
You can walk on me.
What am I?
- candy
- <u>snow</u>
- rain

We are alive.
We can eat and grow.
We have faces and eyes.
What are we?
- <u>children</u>
- flowers
- stones

I am a toy.
I have two tires.
You can ride me.
What am I?
- a boat
- a train
- <u>a bike</u>

ANSWER KEYS: 42, 43, 44, 45

Name _____ Standard: Riddles
DIRECTIONS: Read the riddle in each box. Underline the word that answers each riddle.

I have hands. I have a face. You use me to tell time. What am I?	a kitten <u>a watch</u> a dinner
I push kites high in the sky. I blow on you. You can not see me. What am I?	the sun a cloud <u>the wind</u>
I am something to eat. I am good for you. You eat me in the morning. What am I?	<u>breakfast</u> lunch dinner
I am in your house. I am in your school. You can sit on me. What am I?	a store a horse <u>a chair</u>
I am a boy. I am part of your family. I am not your father. Who am I?	mother <u>brother</u> sister

42

Name _____ Standard: Words in Sentences
DIRECTIONS: Read the riddle in each box. Underline the word that answers each riddle.

I am something you can do. I am done at night. I am done in bed. What am I?	<u>sleep</u> run give
I am in your house. I am not alive. You can watch me. What am I?	a baby a window <u>a TV</u>
I am in the back. Many animals have me. Sometimes I can wag. What am I?	<u>a tail</u> a nose a coat
I am green. I live outside in your yard. You walk and play on me. What am I?	a frog a car <u>grass</u>
I am a white light. I am up in the sky. You can only see me at night. What am I?	the sun <u>a star</u> a bird

43

Name _____ Standard: Following Directions
DIRECTIONS: Read the sentences then do what they say.

Here are three balls. Color the middle one blue. Draw an X on the first one. Color the last one green.	
Here are two cars. Circle the big car. Color the little car red. Color the big car yellow.	
Here are four birds. Draw an X on the first bird. Circle the last bird. Put a 2 on the second bird.	
Here are two boxes. Draw another box. Color the first box orange. Circle the box you drew.	
Here is a girl. Draw a smile on the girl. Color her hair brown. Put an X next to the girl.	

44

Name _____ Standard: Following Directions
DIRECTIONS: Read the sentences then do what they say.

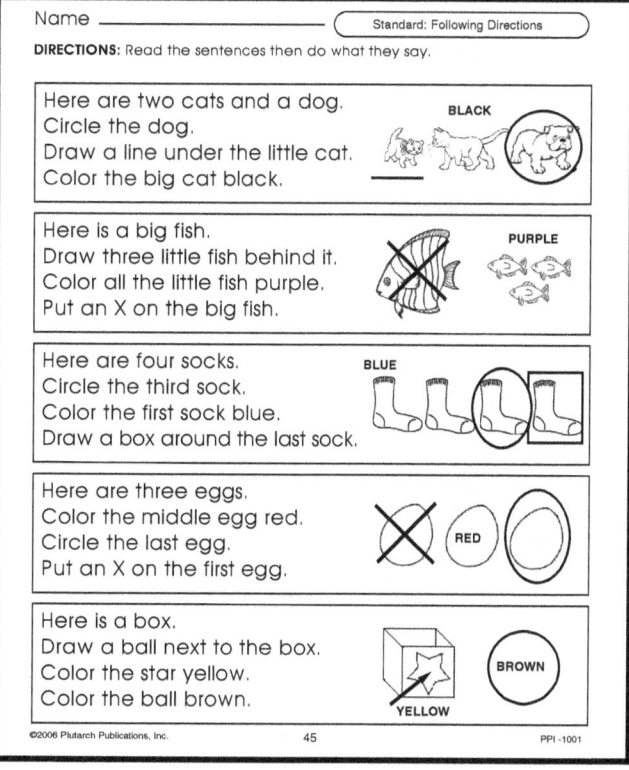

Here are two cats and a dog. Circle the dog. Draw a line under the little cat. Color the big cat black.	
Here is a big fish. Draw three little fish behind it. Color all the little fish purple. Put an X on the big fish.	
Here are four socks. Circle the third sock. Color the first sock blue. Draw a box around the last sock.	
Here are three eggs. Color the middle egg red. Circle the last egg. Put an X on the first egg.	
Here is a box. Draw a ball next to the box. Color the star yellow. Color the ball brown.	

45

©2008 Plutarch Publications, Inc. PPI-1001

ANSWER KEYS: 46, 47, 48, 49

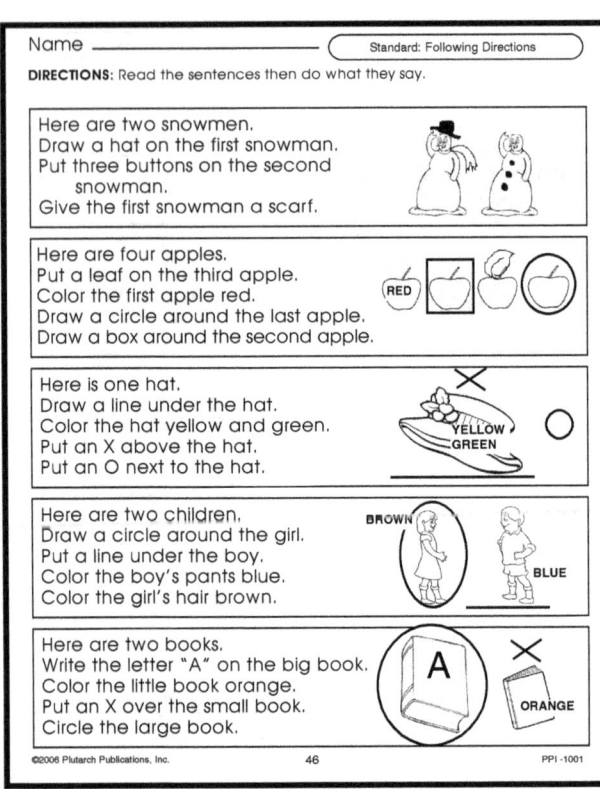

ANSWER KEYS: 50, 51, 52, 53

ANSWER KEYS: 54, 55, 56, 57

Name _____ Standard: Narrative Stories
DIRECTIONS: Read the story then answer the questions.

My Pet
I have a pet rabbit. His name is Puff. He has a fluffy tail and long ears. I take him for a walk every day. We play together. He is a nice pet.

1. What is the name of this story?
   The name of the story is My Pet.
2. What kind of animal is my pet?
   The pet is a rabbit.
3. What is the name of my pet?
   The name of the rabbit is Puff.
4. What two things does Puff have?
   Puff has a fluffy tail and long ears.
5. Where do I take Puff every day?
   I take Puff for a walk every day.
6. What can Puff and I do together?
   We play together.
7. What kind of pet would you like to have?
   answers will vary

Name _____ Standard: Narrative Stories
DIRECTIONS: Read the story then answer the questions.

Playing Together
Matt and Pat played together today. They hit a ball with a bat. They rode their bikes and played with toys in the sandbox. They were tired by dinner time.

1. What is the name of this story?
   The name of the story is Playing Together.
2. Who played together?
   Matt and Pat played together.
3. What did they use to hit the ball?
   They hit the ball with a bat.
4. What did Matt and Pat ride?
   They rode their bikes.
5. Where did they play with their toys?
   They played with toys in the sandbox.
6. How did Matt and Pat feel by dinner time?
   Matt and Pat were tired by dinner time.
7. What do you like to play with your friends?
   answers will vary

Name _____ Standard: Narrative Stories
DIRECTIONS: Read the story then answer the questions.

At the Zoo
Our zoo is very nice. The tigers and lions roar. The seals swim and do tricks. Monkeys swing from trees and make faces at us. They make us laugh!

1. What is the name of this story?
   The name of the story is At the Zoo.
2. Which animals can roar?
   Tigers and lions can roar.
3. Which animals do tricks?
   Seals do tricks.
4. What two things can the seals do?
   Seals can swim and do tricks.
5. Which animals swing in the trees?
   Monkeys swing in the trees.
6. Which animals make us laugh?
   Monkeys make us laugh.
7. What is your favorite animal at the zoo?
   answers will vary

Name _____ Standard: Narrative Stories
DIRECTIONS: Read the story then answer the questions.

My Birthday
Today is my birthday. I am six years old! My friends will come to my party. We will play games and eat cake. I will make a wish and blow out the candles. It will be fun.

1. What is the name of this story?
   The name of the story is My Birthday.
2. Why am I having a party today?
   Today is my birthday.
3. How old am I today?
   I am six years old today.
4. Who will come to my party?
   My friends will come to my party.
5. What will we do at the party?
   We will play games and eat cake.
6. When will I make a wish?
   I will make a wish before I blow out the candles.
7. What will you wish for on your birthday?
   answers will vary

ANSWER KEYS: 58, 59, 60. 61

Name _____ Standard: Narrative Stories
DIRECTIONS: Read the story then answer the questions.

Baby Sister

Sue has a new baby sister named Ann. Sue helps Mother with Ann. Sue holds the baby and helps feed her, too. Mother says that Sue is a good big sister for baby Ann.

1. What is the name of this story?
   The name of the story is Baby Sister.
2. Who has a new baby sister?
   Sue has a new baby sister.
3. What is the baby's name?
   The baby's name is Ann.
4. Who does Sue help?
   Sue helps Mother.
5. What two things does Sue do to help?
   Sue holds and feeds the baby.
6. What does Mother say about Sue?
   Sue is a good big sister for Ann.
7. How would you help with a new baby?
   answers will vary

©2006 Plutarch Publications, Inc.   58   PPI-1001

Name _____ Standard: Narrative Stories
DIRECTIONS: Read the poem then answer the questions.

Wake Up!

Baby sister sitting there,
Sleeping in your high chair.
What made you so tired today?
Please wake up. I want to play!

1. What is this poem about?
   The poem is about a sleeping baby.
2. Who is sleeping?
   Baby is sleeping.
3. Why is the baby sleeping?
   The baby is tired.
4. How long has the baby been asleep?
   The poem doesn't say.
5. Why does this person want the baby to wake up?
   They want the baby to play.
6. Is the person speaking a boy or a girl?
   The poem doesn't say.
7. What game might you play with a baby?
   answers will vary

©2006 Plutarch Publications, Inc.   59   PPI-1001

Name _____ Standard: Narrative Stories
DIRECTIONS: Read the poem then answer the questions.

A Bus Ride

Today Grandma and I took a bus to the mall. We waited at the bus stop and soon a big blue bus pulled up. I helped Grandma go up the steps and we sat in the seat behind the driver. There were many people on the bus. It was a fun ride!

1. What is the title of this story?
   The name of the story is A Bus Ride.
2. Where were Grandma and I going?
   We are going to the mall.
3. What color was the bus?
   The bus was blue.
4. In which seat did Grandma and I sit?
   We sat in the seat behind the driver.
5. Where did we wait for the bus?
   We waited at the bus stop.
6. How did I help Grandma?
   I helped Grandma go up the steps.
7. Where would you like to go on a bus?
   answers will vary

©2006 Plutarch Publications, Inc.   60   PPI-1001

Name _____ Standard: Narrative Stories
DIRECTIONS: Read the story then answer the questions.

Friends

Jeff is my best friend. We are both boys. Jeff is tall and I am short. I have brown eyes but Jeff's eyes are blue. I like to run but Jeff likes to climb trees. We are very different, but we have lots of fun together.

1. What is the title of this story?
   The title of the story is Friends.
2. How are Jeff and I alike?
   Jeff and I are both boys.
3. Who is taller, Jeff or me?
   Jeff is taller than me.
4. What color are my eyes?
   My eyes are brown.
5. Who likes to climb trees?
   Jeff likes to climb trees.
6. Which boy has a dog for a pet?
   The story doesn't say.
7. Who is your best friend?
   answers will vary

©2006 Plutarch Publications, Inc.   61   PPI-1001

ANSWER KEYS: 62, 63, 64, 65

Name _____ Standard: Narrative Stories
DIRECTIONS: Read the story then answer the questions.

Helping the Family

Jean has a large family. There are many things that need to be done. Jean helps by making her bed every morning before school. She sets the table for dinner every night. She reads to her little brother, too. Jean helps her family by doing her jobs well.

1. What is the title of this story?
   The title of the story is Helping the Family.

2. Who is this story about?
   This story is about Jean.

3. How many jobs does Jean have?
   Jean has three jobs.

4. What job does Jean do in the morning?
   Jean makes her bed every morning.

5. What is Jean's job at dinner time?
   She sets the table for dinner.

6. How many people are in Jean's family?
   The story doesn't say. (May infer "5" from picture)

7. How do you think Jean's jobs help her family?
   answers will vary

Name _____ Standard: Nonfictional Stories
DIRECTIONS: Read the story then answer the questions.

Plants

Plants are living things. They have roots, stems, and leaves. The stem is the part that holds up the plant. The roots and leaves gather rain and sun to make food. Many of the foods we eat come from plants.

1. What is this story about?
   This story is about plants.

2. How many parts does a plant have?
   Plants have three parts.

3. What are the three parts of a plant?
   The roots, stem, and leaves are parts of a plant.

4. How do the roots and leaves help the plant?
   They gather rain and sun to make food.

5. Which part holds up the plant?
   The stem holds up the plant.

6. Are plants alive?
   Yes. Plants are living things.

7. Name a food that comes from a plant.
   answers will vary

Name _____ Standard: Nonfictional Stories
DIRECTIONS: Read the story then answer the questions.

Matter

Matter is anything that has weight and takes up space. Matter can be solid like your desk, liquid like water, or gas like the air. Everything around us is matter. We are matter, too!

solid
liquid
gas

1. What is the topic of this story?
   The story topic is matter.

2. What is matter?
   It is anything that has weight and takes up room.

3. Name the three types of matter.
   Three types of matter are solid, liquid and gas.

4. What kind of matter is milk?
   Milk is a liquid.

5. What kind of matter is a box?
   A box is a solid.

6. Is a book solid, liquid, or gas matter?
   A book is solid matter.

7. Water is a liquid. What kind of matter is ice?
   Ice is solid matter.

Name _____ Standard: Nonfictional Stories
DIRECTIONS: Read the story then answer the questions.

Senses

People smell with noses, hear with ears, taste with tongues, feel with skin, and see with eyes. These five things are called senses and they help us learn about our world.

smell
hear
taste
feel
see

1. What is the topic of this story?
   The topic of this story is senses.

2. How many senses do people have?
   People have five senses.

3. Which sense uses our eyes?
   We use our eyes to see. (Sight)

4. Which part of our body helps us hear?
   Our ears help us hear.

5. Which part of our body helps us smell?
   Our noses help us smell.

6. Why do we need senses?
   Senses help us learn about the world.

7. Which sense do you like to use the most?
   answers will vary

ANSWER KEYS: 66, 67, 68, 69

Name _____ *Standard: Nonfictional Stories*
DIRECTIONS: Read the story then answer the questions.

The Night Sky

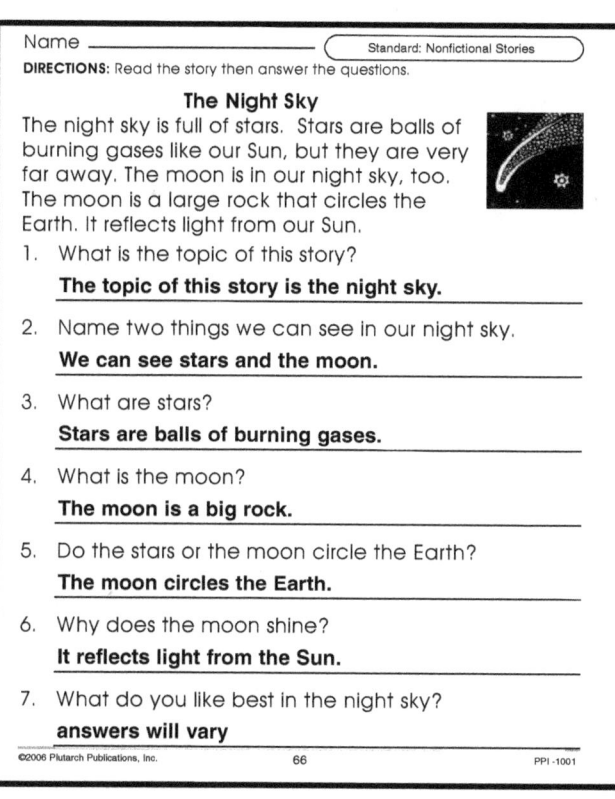

The night sky is full of stars. Stars are balls of burning gases like our Sun, but they are very far away. The moon is in our night sky, too. The moon is a large rock that circles the Earth. It reflects light from our Sun.

1. What is the topic of this story?
   The topic of this story is the night sky.
2. Name two things we can see in our night sky.
   We can see stars and the moon.
3. What are stars?
   Stars are balls of burning gases.
4. What is the moon?
   The moon is a big rock.
5. Do the stars or the moon circle the Earth?
   The moon circles the Earth.
6. Why does the moon shine?
   It reflects light from the Sun.
7. What do you like best in the night sky?
   answers will vary

Name _____ *Standard: Nonfictional Stories*
DIRECTIONS: Read the story then answer the questions.

Weather

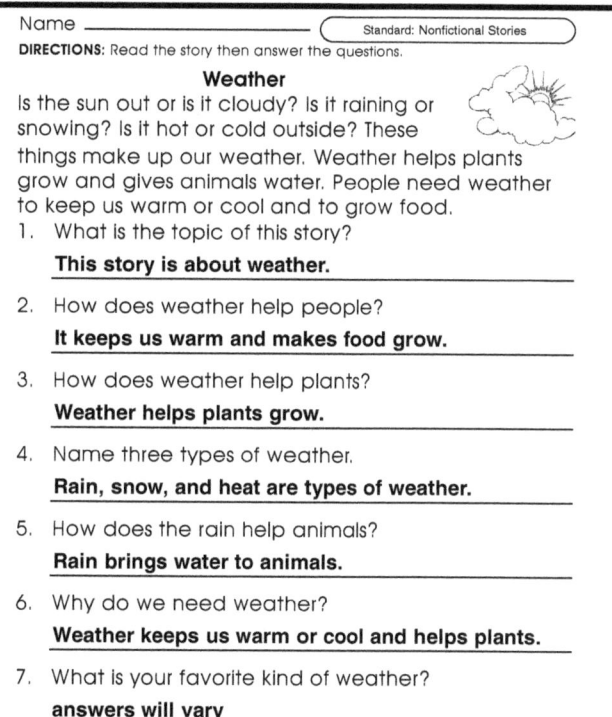

Is the sun out or is it cloudy? Is it raining or snowing? Is it hot or cold outside? These things make up our weather. Weather helps plants grow and gives animals water. People need weather to keep us warm or cool and to grow food.

1. What is the topic of this story?
   This story is about weather.
2. How does weather help people?
   It keeps us warm and makes food grow.
3. How does weather help plants?
   Weather helps plants grow.
4. Name three types of weather.
   Rain, snow, and heat are types of weather.
5. How does the rain help animals?
   Rain brings water to animals.
6. Why do we need weather?
   Weather keeps us warm or cool and helps plants.
7. What is your favorite kind of weather?
   answers will vary

Name _____ *Standard: Reading Maps*
DIRECTIONS: Use the map to answer the questions.

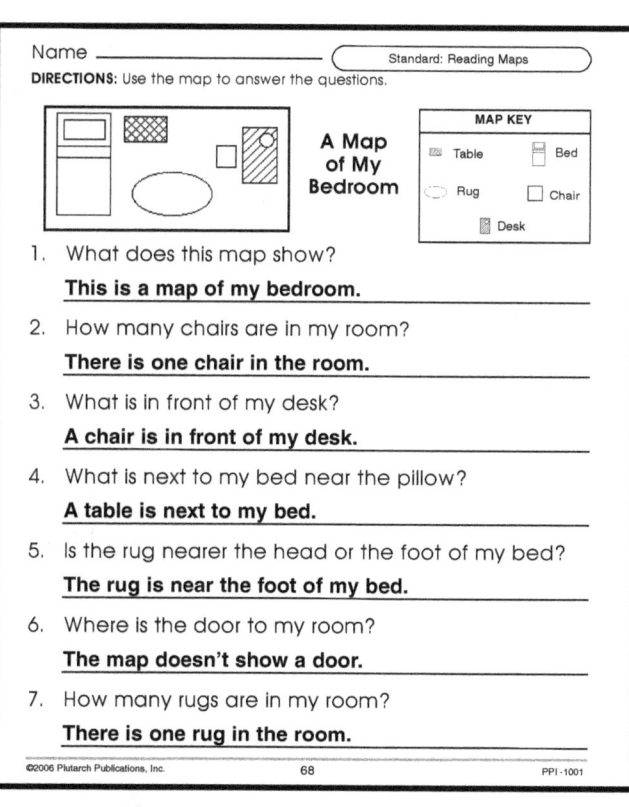

A Map of My Bedroom

MAP KEY: Table, Bed, Rug, Chair, Desk

1. What does this map show?
   This is a map of my bedroom.
2. How many chairs are in my room?
   There is one chair in the room.
3. What is in front of my desk?
   A chair is in front of my desk.
4. What is next to my bed near the pillow?
   A table is next to my bed.
5. Is the rug nearer the head or the foot of my bed?
   The rug is near the foot of my bed.
6. Where is the door to my room?
   The map doesn't show a door.
7. How many rugs are in my room?
   There is one rug in the room.

Name _____ *Standard: Reading Maps*
DIRECTIONS: Use the map to answer the questions.

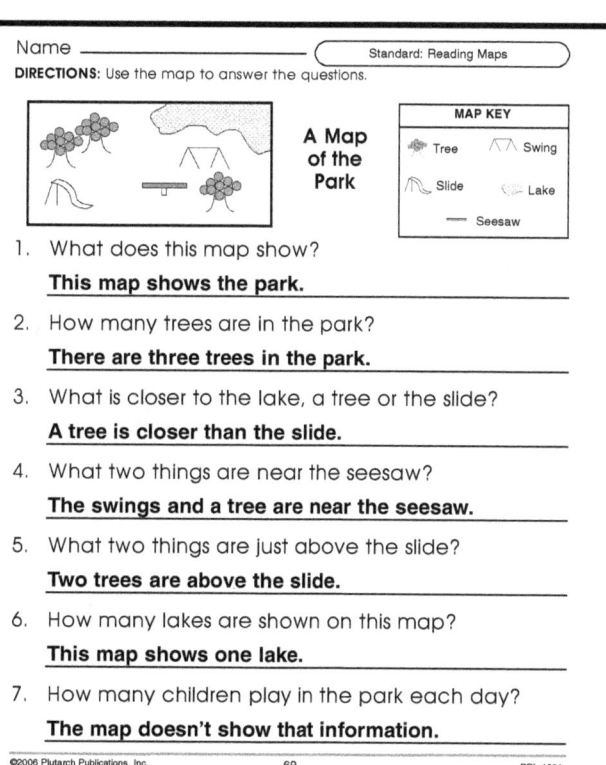

A Map of the Park

MAP KEY: Tree, Swing, Slide, Lake, Seesaw

1. What does this map show?
   This map shows the park.
2. How many trees are in the park?
   There are three trees in the park.
3. What is closer to the lake, a tree or the slide?
   A tree is closer than the slide.
4. What two things are near the seesaw?
   The swings and a tree are near the seesaw.
5. What two things are just above the slide?
   Two trees are above the slide.
6. How many lakes are shown on this map?
   This map shows one lake.
7. How many children play in the park each day?
   The map doesn't show that information.

www.ingramcontent.com/pod-product-compliance
Lightning Source LLC
Chambersburg PA
CBHW081018040426
42444CB00014B/3254